ANONYMOUS
in the
TOWN
THAT TALKS

CONSTANTINE O'DONNELL

Copyright © 2021 Constantine O'Donnell

All rights reserved. No part of this book may be reproduced, stored, or transmitted by any means—whether auditory, graphic, mechanical, or electronic—without written permission of both publisher and author, except in the case of brief excerpts used in critical articles and reviews. Unauthorized reproduction of any part of this work is illegal and is punishable by law.

ISBN: 978-1-63950-055-0 (sc)
ISBN: 978-1-63950-056-7 (e)

Because of the dynamic nature of the Internet, any web addresses or links contained in this book may have changed since publication and may no longer be valid. The views expressed in this work are solely those of the author and do not necessarily reflect the views of the publisher, and the publisher hereby disclaims any responsibility for them.

Writers Apex

Gateway Towards Success

8063 MADISON AVE #1252
Indianapolis, IN 46227
+13176596889
www.writersapex.com

FOREWORD

This book is the culmination of my entire life's work in poetry (that I've kept!). I started writing first in a fit of anger at my Father, making me work extra shifts in our bar and restaurant. His response then of me getting angry at him when he thought I was out of line drove me insane. I was 16. My writing felt therapeutic, and I never really had any real intention of writing a book of poetry. I threw the majority of it away in the beginning, firstly for fear he'd read it and then out of lack of respect for my own ability. I then heard in later years an urban tale of Bono picking Fairytales of New York scrunched in a ball out of Shane McGowans waste basket as he lay drunk on the bed(if this is indeed true and not an urban myth!!). That ended that, I've kept everything I have possibly ever written since. At the beginning, as I wrote, I used to rip the paper of my A4 sheets with my pen; such was the frustration. I first wrote in a tirade, then as I calmed, I started to get it to rhyme. It was funny after a while. The therapy idea came from a programme I had watched on TV that said putting what was annoying you down on paper helped you get it out. No one ever has to read it. You can throw it away. My father caught me writing a while after I began in my room one day and told me, "never write anything down you don't want to be read," and that is what I have done.

The poetry is autobiographical, and the main content is made up of my unjust incarceration in mental asylums in Ireland.

There is a lot of love in there, too, and loadsa humour.

It goes from my very early works, so you can see the progression. I hope it inspires all of you to put pen to paper! Enjoy!

Slainte,

Con

CONTENTS

Love 1

Fulfillment..........................2
The Moon...........................2
Briona 3
Lives...................................3
Forore 4
The day before 4
The day after.....................4
My darling.........................4
Cling to her, ha!................5
What lies within 5
Mirth 6
Strewn 6
Trance................................6
Mind..................................7
Grateful.............................7
Ma petite cherie 7
Unknown 8

Earth 11

Rise aith a View...............12
Never Again! 12
Curtains 12
Drink................................13
Lost and found 13
Verbose 14
No regrets 14
Received?.........................14
Safety in numbers 15
Fight 15
Sink in!.............................16
The Squall 16

The Irish Way..................17
W.A.B.C 18
Windows..........................19
Cure..................................19
Hitchhike.........................19
Truly.................................20
Drugs cause harm of Atom sure ..20
Life....................................20
Ni Neart go cur le cheile 21
ThrowAway Our Note 21
News from home 22
Greens...............................22
Armaggedon 22
Brown paper bag..............23
First impressions..............23
Ancestral Intelligence.................24
A thought.........................25
The Beautiful mind 25
Abounds...........................25
Advantage 26
Homeless..........................26
Torridness 27
Cliffs no Moher 27
The Chain 27
Insert.................................28
Line it 28
Mysteries..........................29
'69......................................29
All an illusion..................29
O'Douls 29
Palates 30
They're out to Annoy 30
Shitzo Diverse..................30

Your Pie Hole	31
Leg Before Wicket	31
Flute	32
Fubar	32
Innit	32
The lost poem	33
Solace	33
Precise	33
Shoulders for boulders	33
Christmas	34
Fire	34
Yoga	34
Yoga for Celine	35
Life not simple	35
Irma	36
Jesus wept	36
DJ	36
Eastumour	37
U	37
Welcome	38
Sprinkle	38
Psalm	38
Gib	38
Letterkenny	39
Sun in the sky with dreams	39
Antibes	39
Dole day	39
Stuck	40
Bridges and fridges	40
Coerced	40
A hundred years have come and gone	41
Axe no questions. Tell no lies	41

St. Pat's Mental Asylum Dublin 43

If dreams could come true	44
I'm	44
Depression	45
War and Peace	45
Nothing	46
Truth	46
University of life	47
Crystal clear	48
Patience	48
Together	49
Crosswords	49
Biomedical material	49
Childs play	50
A song for paradise	50
The Ums	51
Monica	51
The Galway races	52
Kindred Spirits	52
A busy day	53
Just one minute	53
Just the one	54
I don't love Lucky	54
Fitness	54
Give us a few seconds	55
Sown	56
Space	56
Storm in a tea cup	56
Liverpool F.C	57
Favourite things	57
Concert	58
Fran	58
Escape!	59
Bending the rules	59
Relax	60
Believe	60
AA	61
CONcise	61
Gone?	62
I Con	62
Anything	63
Imprisonment	63
Love & Depression	64
Eternal Itch	64
Lots of love Kena	65

Snatchet 65
Fuck the models Kena 65
What attracted you me 2 u? 66
Back to reality? 66
Evolution 67
Golf 67

St. Pat's Mental Asylum 2 – The seroquel 69

Reason? 70
Eileen 70
Irish summers 70
0352hrs.....Bedtime 71
Words of scrabble 71
Sleep 71
Trinity college? 72
Who, me, I...? 72
bUNI-polar 73
Bunnies 73
Cut grass 73
Love won 74
Love 74
Cuckoo 74
Much ado about nothing 74
Sandals 75
The Closet has been deskeletised 75
Party hats 75
Perfect 76
Picture perfect 76
14 lines 76
Horses 77
Trinity 77
Cricket - Trinity 77
Player/Manager 78
Pole 79
The Scooby doo ending 79
Free admission 79
Radiation 80

Scratch 80
Unito 80
Fianna Never Fail 80
Stereo 81
The Office! 81
The happy family law
solicitor who's Bipolar and
recovering from alchoholism 81
Cigarette butts 82
Embalmed 82
It is as it is 82
Borderline 83
Chocolate 84
Coinyabeta 84
Pourqoui pas 85
Super friend/GRASS 85
Swell Waves 85
Therapy? 86
The Wagon 86
Weekender Bender 86
NoName 87
Scaley 87
Catharsis 87
Secret Agent 008 88
The 32 Musketeers 88
The bullshit I was told 89
You are all @ sea 89
3's 89
KowLOonKrazy 89
Teamwork 90
Tree-leaves 90
10/1 90
Autumn 90
Children 90
Clingy 91
Little Hitleress 91
Sexually frustrated 91
Bog roll blues 91
I's 92
Paperback 92

Sarah	92
C'est la vie	92
Musique	93
Turbulence	93
Focus	93
King prawns	94
Five	94
Hear & Now	95
Nail on the head	95
Snakes & Dragons	95
Windolay	96
Animals	96
Lost in Music	97
A kiss	97
Confidence	97
In-between Dreams	97
Psychiatric hospital	98
Road rage	98
Should	98
Fingers	99
Alien Nation	99
Chair	99
CONformity	99
Random Rodent	100
Words	100
Old and why's?	100
Susie	101
The Angelus	101
Elationships	101
The Wild bunch	101
Dog	102
Leaving	102
When I get out	103
Revelation	103
SandyAndy	103
Associates	103
Doggerel	104
Comply	104

Letterkenny mental asylum in Donegal 105

Lazers	106
Fiona	106
Astronautadamus	106
Mother	107
Darkness	107
Happy BD Andrew	107
Timo	108
With Ease	108

Limericks 109

Vomit	110
Fish	110
Food	110
Journey	110
Actors	110
Animal	110
Director	110

LOVE

01/01/00

Fulfillment

Every breath I breathe,
says I love you,
you're the breath that
breathes air to my lungs,
and life to my soul.

Without you, I suffocate,
and with you, I float,
your love is the ocean,
on which I sail my boat.

The more I think of you,
the horizon expands,
to distant countries,
and foreign sands,
places afar,
and also at home,
for my heart is with you,
whenever I roam.

We'll sail our ship,
from shore to shore,
and we will be together,
forevermore.
Our souls will find wind,
where there is none to be found,
and carry us safely along,
the most treacherous sound.

07/03/00

The Moon

Through misty glass,
staring at the moon,
listening to the soft beat,
of my favourite tune,

Thinking of you,
as the clouds drift past,
knowing the darkness,
will not last,

through time and persistence,
the light will shine through,
just like our love,
and my longing for you,

In the shadow again,
as I continue to gaze,
once again, it shines strong,
to dazzle and amaze,

Those who were in
doubt if it would,
are proven wrong,
For in the shadows,
life may cast,
our love will last,
as long as the moon shines on,

The silvery path to eternity,
is where our love never ends,
we will grow old together,
and take what life sends,

To young? To old?
To soon? Too late?
There's no set time,
or given date,

Two souls combined,
can never be parted,
by distance or time,
or waters uncharted,

The join is seamless,
it cannot be found,
like the start of a wave,
or the end of a sound,

From two souls to one,
the journey's begun,
I feel the tingling,
that says you're the one,

I'm the happiest and securest,
that I've ever been,
and when we make love,
you take me to places,
that I've never seen,

I let myself go,
like never before,
and each time we come there,
I want to see more,

The sensation is the most beautiful,
that I've ever felt,
and when I look in your eyes,
I feel my heart melt,

It brings a lump to my throat,
and a tear to my eye,
and all my will,
not to cry

Tears of joy,
for thoughts untold,
but through action and time,
they begin to unfold,

Our love will shine,
in all its glory,
through the test of time,
as a never-ending story!

01/01/01

Briona

Red lips &
hair clips,
& big deep blue eyes,
& wavy mad hair,
with artistic dyes,
that cute sexy laugh,
that so turns me on,
and that puppy dog look,
that says, "Come to bed. Juan,"
the smell of your scent,
the feel of your touch,
These are just some of the reasons,
why I love you so much.

'01

Lives

When watching your face,
I have to stifle my roar,
I can feel it coming,
the blood rush in our veins,
the head on collision,
of two speeding trains,
I squeeze you tight,
you bite my chin,

nothing else in the world matters,
but our feelings within,
the trains collide,
we both explode,
we're floating in space,
with no fixed abode,
the sky is happy,
it screams out Amen,
we're the moon and the sun,
together again,
for eternity.

'01

Forore

You save me from myself,
I'm in love with no-one else,
never could,
never would.

19/01/01

The day before

The excitement inside me,
is starting to build,
the void of not seeing you,
about to be filled,
before it was confirmed,
I could not let it grip,
because I know if I did,
my heart would rip,
disappointments not strong enough,
it's a fate worse than death.

20/01/01

The day after

It finally happened,
I can let out my breath!!

03/02/01

My darling

As my darling wife,
Oh, what a life,
of joy & fun's in store for me,
I'm so satisfied, contented & happy,
with you as my wife to be.

But the life ahead is for both of us,
to love and cherish and share,
And for me the man,
to do what I can,
to smother you with
affection & care.

For you to have what you want,
not just what you need,
to make you safe + happy + loved,
for this - to my last drop, I'd bleed.

But as long as we have,
the love of each other,
we need never worry,
we'll be happy & we'll survive,
should the whole world
turn all BLURRY.

12/04/01

Cling to her, ha!

Thinking of feelings,
do they happen through time?
Or flash in an instant?
And start crowding your mind?
Never wanted someone so badly,
that I can taste and touch and smell,
when I close my eyes and think,
and for a while, I feel so happy,
but when I open, I'm in hell,
I want you here right by my side,
and snuggling in my ear,
so, you feel safe and know
that'll I protect you,
and that you need never have a fear.
I know its hard right at this time,
for me to be away,
but the only consolation is,
that you and I are here to stay!

16/06/01

What lies within

The kiss,
the gift,
the smile,
the yawn,
like the first rays of light,
just at the dawn,

the sense of beginning,
the start of something new,
the turning of blackness,
into blue,

like the spiritual feeling,
after a well said mass,
or the cool smell of freshness,
from a summer evenings cut grass,

dormant emotions beneath my skin,
you brought them out
from deep within,

Heightened awareness of
the beauty around me,
like so many who look,
but do not see,

beneath your beauty,
which is so pleasing to the eyes,
lies so much more hidden,
in disguise,

I've discovered some,
and I want to see more,
you'll never get rid of me,
now you've opened up the door,

I feel your strength,
and I see your resolve,
and I'm honoured there's a part,
for me to involve,

In your life and your future,
in which you'll never tire,
because burning inside you,
is the eternal fire.

19/08/01

Mirth

I'd give you the Earth,
for what it is worth,
Which for me at present,
is shrouded in mirth,
If it was given to me,
With all its money and gold,
All the fortune of wealth,
and secrets unsold,
What kind of people are these?
What grip do they hold?
What is the life in which they hide?
Love & happiness is not something,
that can be bought and sold,
For me, it would mean nothing,
without you at my side.

14/02/02

Strewn

Early morning when I wake,
Within my heart,
I feel a little break,
at the realisation,
that you're not there,
from the vacant space,
where your shapeless hair,
should be beside me,
upon my pillow,
and your beautiful scent
upon the air,
Our limbs a tangle,
that could not be defined,
from the beginning of yours,
to the end of mine,
The warmth of your breath,
upon my chest,
the rise and fall,
of your shapely breasts,
I woke you with a kiss,
and the feeling was bliss,
when you opened your eyes,
and said I love you,
That beaming smile,
that makes everything worthwhile,
with just a hint,
of your cute white teeth,
I was already aroused,
at what lay beneath,
the crumpled quilt,
strewn across the bed,
you slowly exhaled,
then turned your head,
I told you I loved you,
you told me the same,
a forthcoming attraction,
of when we're name and name.

02/03/02

Trance

I kiss both your eyes,
& thank God, for your sight,
can't think what would be,
had you not seen me that night,
A blessing from God,
Is it in disguise?
I think it's a dream,
til I open my eyes,
you had an edge,
you knew me before,
The walls around my fortress,
where brought to the floor,
You broke down the walls,
and smashed through the door,

I stood there defenseless,
caught in the headlamps,
my heart couldn't be slowed,
by a thousand speed ramps,
The curves of your body,
and the zany dance,
a sight to behold,
that left me in a trance,
the trance isn't broken,
it will long remain,
a beautiful memory,
imprinted on my brain.

06/05/02

Mind

Another day closer to you,
Is how I feel with everything I do,
If it passes the time,
and occupies my mind,
then I'll do it,
just to ease the longing for you.

11/02/02

Grateful

I'm grateful for what I've got,
not jealous for what I've not,
And for this, I feel truly blessed,
Not wanting like the
eternally obsessed,
Only happy when they're
complaining,
"It's because of this...",
they are always explaining,
Well, I found my love
to be my wife,
and will always be happy
with her in my life.

09/09/04

I wrote this about Jamima.

Ma petite cherie

I feel it lifting, but I'm
taking it slow,
no more leaping before I know,
I have the laughter of a grafter,
but my banters at a canter,
I'm reading the rhyming dictionary,
and playing mental pictionary,
my scribbles at a dribble,
but I want to hear it roar,
I want to be happy,
I want to be me,
I want to feel companionship,
that'll set me free,
less than half my life,
without a wife,
but who is this girl?
My fantasy....?!
Without a boast, there
is many that care,
but that which attracted me
was non-conformity,
it gave them hope,
some dispelled the rope.
I changed their outlook on reality,
But I am lost and feel
I can't be found,
I'm trying to find my centre
and touch the ground,
I touch the earth, but
can't feel the taste,
surely all I've done is not a waste,
I've lived a movie in my
own mind's eye,
I'm on the brink of a crossroads,

and I don't know why?
I'm on a trampoline with
mile long springs,
waiting to rise and test
my kevlar wings,
I don't want to miss it,
what a terrible fear,
is my life on hold?
What am I waiting to clear?
The smoke I've created,
is blinding my eyes,
my heart wants to move on
but maintain the ties,
Love is a bastard,
I love it to death,
I try not to think of her
with every breath,
this isn't her fault, and
neither is it mine,
but in the truth,
there is wine.
It's all my will trying not to
spill this all out into a glass,
it would be nice with a
few cubes of ice,
but it was her that capped the gas.
My spirit was escaping
with no anticipating,
wandering it blew into
a paranoid wind,
as long as the juice was
there, I did not care,
I could squeeze from any excuse,
all rhyme no reason
whatever the season,
I was just brimming to let
all hell break loose,
So, I calm the edge with
an eternal pledge,
and use her as my muse,
but I didn't mask,
did she want the task,
is that why I fumble and
stumble and confuse?
Am I writing history in a
man-made mystery?
To which the answer eludes?
And every time it hurts,
in fits and spurts,
I can't blame the frustration
that intrudes,
She's stated her case, face to face,
but why do I see eyes
that are hidden?
For if the truth that I
feel is actually real,
then God, please let them
do their bidding,
or is it all fake?
And I just keep stepping
on that rake,
oblivious to reputation and pride,
but I wish it so,
that we'll stand toe to toe,
and eye to eye as
husband and bride.

06/07/05

Unknown

Somethings they go unnoticed,
some things they go unchanged,
why do I get the feeling,
of always being estranged?
Unknown in my lifetime,
but maybe known all along,
these people actually care for me,
how could I have been so wrong?
The hungry emotion,

that eats within,
nibbles and bites,
I wish it only ate sin.
The vividness of memories,
triggered from the vibes,
I hope the good ones win,
I'm weakened by the jibes.
I have the strength,
but it's in reserve,
I'll give her the devotion,
Of that she deserves,
But I hate this Yeats shit,
and the thing about Maud Gonne,
Her name is Flo,
And my name is Juan,
I've walked towards the edge,
and stood on tip-toes
while standing there,
I'm reaching out into life,
and I know that it's not fair,
I've become a little paranoid,
where a glance can
seem like a stare,
I need the arms of one true heart,
to reach out and comfort me,
I wish this outward weakness,
didn't need a key.
But there it is, so get a grip,
and deal with it in the way you can,
listen to the spirits that have
always guided you,
I'd rather hear the truth,
to satisfy the plan,
my heads not up,
and in the clouds,
and not beneath the ground,
I'll not beg,
but I'll keep my love,
for the one that I have found.

EARTH

18/09/99

Rise aith a View

Early morning rise,
the Sun in my eyes,
the brightness in the light,
sets the clouds on fire,
and lays a golden path,
on a sea that's swelling higher.
No matter if you stand or sit,
your perspective or your view,
the mood for the day is always set,
just like the morning tune!

16/02/01

Never Again!

It's always the scene,
seems like I've always been,
here a hundred times before,
There's obviously a reason,
This is probably the case,
Whole body is tired,
eyes sprayed with mace.
Call it a hangover,
Call it needin' a cure,
Whatever way you look at it,
life still looks a blur,
Both through the eyes,
and through the mind,
every little task,
seems like a bind,
Another few hours,
will dissipate the pain,
with the immortal words,
never again!

'01

Curtains

Unbridled, bedazzled,
slightly half frazzled,
fuzzy brain feels the pain,
of a night that was razzled.
Now to open the blind,
that's a curtain of a kind,
and let the world looking in,
show me where to begin,
watchin you, watchin me,
a vague apparition that I see,
there's no solid definition,
so, it joins in the melee,
for the performance to start,
the curtain is undrawn,
it's been hanging around waiting,
since the early dawn,
so, don't keep them restless,
or you'll be seen as a pawn,
a sheep through your life,
with an incessant bleat,
not able to stand,
on your own two feet,
Right! You black sheep,
have you any wool?
Position's, please!
Not one amongst us,
is a fool.
Open the curtains,
we'll wash them over like a wave,
then sit back, feet up,
and let the reviews rave!

16/04/01

Drink

Drink when you're happy,
Drink when you're sad,
Drink when you're lonely,
Drink when you're mad,
Drink when you're worried,
Drink when you're scared,
Drink to feel good,
Drink to feel better,
Drinking the beer,
Slowly opening the letter,
good news or bad?
Will he? Or won't he?
Don't mind him,
he's Jack the lad,
loves to be loved,
centre of it all,
running out of chances,
breaking down the wall,
the wall is unstable,
cracks starting to show,
so much to lose,
learning to slow,
not as smart,
so much to learn,
of older and wiser,
keep an eye on my stern,
only one answer,
the answer is plain,
learn to control,
if not, then abstain,
can't control,
when the mind is in a frame,
think of it now,
causes pain,
light in the tunnel,
an oncoming train?
Keep mind focused,
strong on the goal,
think of my girl,
look into my soul,
are you the man,
or are you a mouse?
Go to it,
and do it,
think of your house,
stand up and be counted,
must look after her soul,
guard with your life,
and you'll end up on pole.

07/05/01

Lost and found

Some say I'm crazy,
some say I'm mad,
maybe cause I've only ever
listened to my Dad,
I say what I think,
And think what I feel,
only cause I know these
feelings are real,
It's the way I always was,
And the way I'll always be,
I lost it for a while but
found it on the sea.
Some listen to rumours,
Some people create them,
I do neither,
and for that some people hate me,
But knowledge is power,
let them think me a fool,
we'll see in the end just
who is the tool.
I've got many great friends,
but there is only a few,

whom I'd lay down my life
for if things went askew.
They know who they are,
it never has to be said,
I know they feel the same,
Otherwise, we'd all be dead.
Some say money,
weekends going out,
But I think love and friendship,
is what life is all about.

02/02/02

Verbose

They've cut my head off as it stands,
I'm playing the Chess
game with no hands.
But they'll grow back,
of that I'm sure,
and with them a perspective
that's clear and pure,
but where do I take advice from,
to do what I believe?
It's my independent mind,
I want to retrieve it.
I've so much to say,
but who wants to hear,
lies that are true,
inside this stratosphere.
People soon tire of stories,
if they think you're
beginning to boast,
so, I'll stick to the normal
moral dilemmas,
of which there are the most.

02/03/02

No regrets

No regrets?
I do fret!
Good or bad decisions???
Bad because I forget,
Remember to great times,
laughter & fun,
oh, what potential,
if we only had the Sun,
The Sun in the sky,
or the one here on Earth?
The close-knit community,
the family as one,
The extended family,
has retracted in size,
Or is it the perspective,
of a part-time out-siders eyes?
More of an effort,
will regain what is lost,
Because of the spirit we had,
should be kept at all costs.

02/06/02

Received?

What do you believe?
The question's asked,
is the answer received?
Do I know?
Or don't I care?
All those questions,
with no answer,
has the drink got a grip,
or can I rip,
free from the noose,
that it holds me in?

Am I ashamed?
Is it a sin?
Of course, I am,
but is it the time,
we're living in?
So many around me,
drink the same,
how can you judge,
with them in the same vain?
My mind is strong,
but will it remain?
Only I know it will,
because I'm so thick,
possibly because I'm a
straight country hick!!!

'02

Safety in numbers

My safe, your safe,
we're all safe together,
how safe is safe?
Your safe or my safe?
Lucky safe stroked,
that bit of white heather,
life can be funny,
and that blood can be runny,
thought I as he ate,
the feet of the bunny,
the luckier I practice,
the luckier I get!
You'll never meet one
luckier than me,
I am the one,
you'll never forget!

06/09/02

Fight

Now when do you fight?
When do you see?
The look in the eye?
The shoulders that flee?
The stimulus required,
the thran and the attacked,
the turn of the cheek,
the look of the meek,
The blind leading the blind,
the guards in the mix,
the throwing of beds,
the tables askew,
the airwaves turning,
the colour of blue,
the wrist, the light,
the giver of bright,
the succumb,
the wall,
the headbanging,
the tall,
the shallow,
the hall,
the fall,
the ground,
the hit,
the teeth,
the bit,
Sit!

31/08/03

Sink in!

Once again,
it happens in place,
you've done it once more,
yer a fucking disgrace,
you've let yourself down,
not to mention all of us,
you're like an open wound,
seaming with puss.
A wound that won't heal,
can you sit still for a second?
And let it fucking seal.
My mind is always racing,
I don't expect you to understand.
I don't, or I'm not like
everyone else,
fit in and be normal,
be like everyone else,
please become bland,
but for me, that's sinking sand,
up to the neck,
just the level that changes,
it moves in minimal ranges,
I love my family and friends,
but fuck the rest,
let them take up diving,
and get the benz.
I'll me be,
cos I love me!!!

23/11/03

I had just started a new job in the North Sea as Second Officer. I did not take over ownership from my father of our family run Seafood bar and restaurant. I wanted to travel the world freely. I had been in a terrible car crash and was being bullied on-board. I was on a bit of a downer - to say the least!

The Squall

Lying in limbo, books on the shelf,
more interest in learning
about my inner self,
sense of direction like a
confused Sea and swell,
look good on the outside,
but all is not well,
self-confidence, motivation,
single-mindedness, and goal,
are lost at present, and it's
damaging my soul,
from all the right moves and
brimming with zest,
a lust for life that was
a "no-contest,"
they're simmering beneath,
just waiting to shine,
but I need a stage that
is rightfully mine,
a stage that's not handed to me
but earned through time,
with respect, hard work, and
being straight down the line,
above all else to thine
own self be true,
is a statement I've held close,
but not always adhered too,
playing the wide boy,
games that aren't mine,
taking measurement from
other's is surely a sign,
I've not strayed far, but
far enough to hurt,

the ones closest to me and
especially myself,
paranoia, self-doubt,
states alien to me,
they aren't readily apparent,
only a few can see,
as a young boy, a teenager,
and now a man,
was, still is, a belief of greatness
in my destiny's hand,
my character is strong, maybe
not as vocal as some,
but my spirits not broken,
and they've far from won.
My time to shines not arrived,
but it will come,
I just hope I see it,
and I've not let it past,
Was it the 'Drunken Duck' bar?
Was that my last?
This is not my belief,
but can't help the what if's,
it sounds like backtracking,
a severe quavering of decision,
that was once so stiff,
I'll miss the attention and
being the star of the show,
something I crave but
at least I know,
now for a substitute,
that earns equal respect,
no begrudging of success
or eternal regrets,
don't listen to others, to
thine own self be true,
sail by your own compass like
you were taught to do,
Fuck'em!!!
aye
Fuck'em!!!

31/07/04

The Irish Way

It all started on the Jeanie Johnston,
when the metamorphosis occurred,
for a brief moment in time,
my whole life was blurred,
the thoughts of the universe,
where blowing my mind,
thinking of the future,
and my fellow mankind,
But after some time,
it started to make sense,
the compression in my head,
became ever denser,
but when fully compressed,
it made room for more,
freed up some space,
and opened up the door,
the path to enlightenment,
became a solid entity for travel,
and the secrets of life,
began to unravel,
success in the distance,
but learn from the past,
a concrete foundation is needed,
for the road to last,
Experience is everything,
So, take heed of all advice,
whether a long-winded suggestion,
or succinct and concise,
it's manners to listen,
but you're not obliged
to believe them,
people mean well,
so, don't be too quick to condemn.

06/09/04

Kiltboy and I held up a radio station aged 10

W.A.B.C

I'm sitting on the toilet sun,
thinking of how the day began,
a decade of life has passed us by,
but there's so much out
there left to try,
enough to stop the
boredom and cry,
situations to get out of intact,
let's go to the station in the
caravan and distract,
and foul is fair and fair is foul,
we'll raise a shit storm,
with our 0.22 trowel,
first, you tell us,
we can write our names,
and true to form, we
begin our games,
till all that is left is a pissed off DJ,
and the big black letter's saying
JUAN & KILTBOY,
Throw us out?
Annoy at your pearl!
But you've done it now,
so there's no going back,
Our little hatched plan
of destruction,
was just put firmly on track,
with misdirection,
we acquired the gun,
but who's gonna point it?
As we fought one on one,
so Kiltboy psyched the
hell out of me,
telling me, I've got a brilliant kick,
Stealthfully through the
first open door,
slick listening out for
the talking tard,
I blasted the studio open,
Kiltboy shouted, "freeze
ya bastard!",
Happy with a job well done,
as he fell apart at the
sight of the gun,
there's the bigman,
shitless wonder now,
mooin over the airwaves,
like a cow,
misdirection puts the
gun back in place,
then off to some mischief,
we do race.
Till the day we die,
we never forget his face,
We'll have plenty of
more stories to tell,
but it's really like a bottomless well,
So, that was one of the
stories of fun,
but they aren't over yet,
not by a million billion
barrels and then some!

'04

I was writing this poem just after I got out of St. Pat's, the second admission. As I was on my bed writing it, it's at that point my Dad put his head around my bedroom door and said "are you at that writing craic again?!" "You know that's the next step back to the mental!!" If you've read iCon, you may remember that point.

Windows

Framed at every corner,
no matter where you turn,
for all the right reasons,
I'm forever less than taciturn.
Your field of vision is always stable,
whatever happens within the view?
From the changing of the seasons,
to life's characters which
you construe.
Moving closer to the pane,
the lifeguard of your soul,
it's who you are,
not what you do,
beyond your reason and control.
Peripherals now inspected,
what's there was there before,
it's just you didn't see it,
while standing at the door.
If you look to see close up,
eyes open, taking in,
you learn to see while
standing back,
the different sounds within the din.
Occidental, Oriental,
North and South,
each has all the traits,
it's the nature of the lookers,
that decide on all their fates.

07/07/05

Cure

I'm happy,
I'm excited,
I resist the overcoming joy,
I'm glad to be alive,
What a lucky boy.
Ain't life wonderful,
ain't life great?
My true character on form,
is a permanent trait,
I feel it rising slowly,
pure and sure,
people that care,
are a definite cure.

17/07/05

Hitchhike

These thoughts I've inside me,
my inner sanctum, my space,
expressions within me,
see the look on my face,
it can be a mask of deception,
to throw you off the scent,
and keep them all guessing,
of my true intent,
if you show your hand too early,
it beggar's belief,
that who you thought you knew,
will go outta their way
to give you grief.
From one point to another,
the shortest distance is curved,
to remove blocks from your path,
you gotta throw a ball
that is swerved,

the road is a long one,
that we hitchhike along,
just remember who lifts you,
and you can't go wrong.

18/07/05

Truly

With all this love inside,
contained beneath the surface,
I'll never run and hide,
my moods never level,
I'm either up or down,
but whatever the state,
you'll never see me frown,
I'll meet you with a smile,
if my words have escaped.

07/08/05

Drugs cause harm of Atom sure

A quiet face is no disgrace,
when you're feeling
out of sorts,
and don't think it's strange,
if you feel a change,
in the attention of
everyone's retorts.
If you're among friends,
it never depends,
on every moment what they think,
just sit there quietly and
accept the warmth,
that's shared from the
odd little wink.
An affection displayed,
is often enough,

because not everything
you always agree upon,
but friends that are real
and have your intentions at heart,
don't look for weakness to exploit.
They look for your strengths
and your weaknesses
that hide,
and build them up,
from the inside,
but if they're destructive
and not the same as you,
then your jib you have to slew,
you need a perspective
that's the same
as your own,
one that'll help you
and with whom you've grown.

'06

Life

I am the greatest,
I am the best,
back me into a corner,
and I'll end your quest.
With every inch of my body,
and every thought in my mind,
I'll fight tooth and nail,
until I'm deaf, dumb, and blind,
If it's a test of strength,
and you want a real fight,
try stopping the sunshine
from turning into night,
if it's a jealous attack that's
to try and whittle down,
then you'll always wear the head,
that's too big for the crown.
A reactive response,

to the threat you perceive,
will leave you entangled,
in the web that you weave.
When you look to yourself,
at the threat that's within,
basic instincts of survival,
is where to begin.
Resentment of control,
and fear of its loss,
is a meal you feel made tastier,
by an inadequate bitter sauce.
Indigestion,
then congestion,
followed when not chewed,
so when offered a slice,
of friendly advice,
think from where it's viewed.

30/01/06

Ní Neart go cur le cheile

The Spartans fell like
leaves from the sky,
so defiant in death,
they did not die,
their remains sowed the seeds,
for generations to come,
to unite as a Nation,
and Stand alone as One.
Basically unique,
their system was designed,
to use fear of the unknown,
as a communal bind,
excellence was encouraged,
men knew their place in a marriage,
and wise words from a woman,
they would never disparage,
They fought for preservation,
and taught common sense,
and when they had a common goal,
they didn't sit on the fence.
They had pride with temperance,
all information was pooled,
and as a nation,
they were destined,
to be wisely ruled.
Their kings were the bravest,
and compassionate among all,
who fought from the front,
with the ANCESTRAL call.

18/02/06

ThrowAway Our Note

You have the right to a yes,
You have a right to a no,
You have the right to ponder,
Or go with the flow,
So, get off the fence,
and stop spouting cents,
that's designed to intrigue,
by causing fatigue,
firing imaginations with
great wealth and gold,
and how everything beneath
heaven can always be sold,
it's a seller's market,
we're always being told,
so, let's give them a creation,
that's 3 in 1 bold.
We'll fire their brains from
great distance and length,
an up-heavel so taciturn that their
reticence will lose strength,
we'll dangle the angle and show
them the square of the hair,
and as the cube of the tube
goes scoobadoobdoob,

we'll dance our jig on our
universal Rubix lube.
We're slippy and sliddy
and all out good fun,
but always remember
one thing about us,
We'll never turn and run!

02/06/06

News from home

Feeling depressed,
feeling so sad,
need to be brought up,
news from home. I'll do it,
even if it's bad,
These words aren't true,
Better good news,
than no news,
bad news is worse,
so these words are only a curse.

06/06/06

Greens

There's a house in the clearing
dyed green with effect,
it's on the wrong cycle,
What do you expect?
Water tumbles from the roof
of our neglected stall,
completing rotation
that's not basic to all.
The broken fountain pen drinks,
from the poisoned ink well,
Finalizing deals of a thirst,
that won't seem to quell.
Born not born,

not force-fed life yet,
alternative thinking,
must be more than a pet.
The diet that's balancing,
chained fastly to excess,
must be given a stability,
that's comfortable with less.
We need a pyramid of thought,
that makes us equilateral,
gives us back our faith
in fellow man,
enough to use each
other as collateral,
an antidote so potent,
it's a permanent vaccine,
and a way of administering
without dilution,
the fear of being clean.
A concentration on the circulation,
of a free windfall of expectation.
Hope has elasticity,
rubber properties that
will erase the pain,
and a spring that keeps rebounding,
when you have everything to gain.

'06

Armaggedon

Is it real?
We see, but we do not feel,
Apathy reigns all
sympathy to the heel.
If you do the right thing,
you're brought to your knees,
and punishment delivered
in various degrees.
Hunger, pollution,
and the Superpowers resistance,

threatens the lifespan,
of our entire existence.
It's a catharsis of dreams,
of people in power,
planted centuries ago,
it's now a withering flower.
The chaotic energy,
of the manmade compression,
the molecular level agitated,
without discretion,
as the compression continues,
the agitation increases,
the friction finds friendships
falling to pieces,
so, unless the voice of the people,
don't sing the same rhyme,
the g(ate) won't stop
the next big bang in time.

'06

Brown paper bag

Would a planet made of granite,
Create its own black hole?
Would the people that
are living there,
have a different soul?
If they had no sky to gaze upon?
Would they let their lives
just move along?
Making money day to day,
only ever stopping to pay?
No sea or tides or wind or rain,
and nothing ever to
cause them pain,
With work and power
their only vice,
and nothing ever to break the ice,
Would they all live in
complete harmony?
All are thinking the same
that they are all free!
Are they any different to him,
or her,
or you,
or me?
When they wonder if
anyone's out there,
that is maybe just the same,
Do their eyes slip from
the scoreboard,
and forget it's all a game?
Is the weight upon their shoulder's,
a little more than they can stand?
But too afraid to ask for help,
they all just say they're grand.
Do their memories have an effect?
When they look forward
with retrospect,
use their experience with intellect,
and share their knowledge
with dialect.
So, if like us,
they have the parts of the sum,
would they all realize
it's a continuum.
That they each shape lives,
even with no wealth,
so why not use it for
everyone's health?

01/07/06

First impressions

When you look at a face,
can you see what's inside?
The secrets beneath,
what does it hide?
Expressions of movement,

language and tone,
a flick of the eyes,
that can cut to the bone.
A smile so radiant,
it could outshine the sun,
or a cheeky little grin,
full of mischief and fun.
The windows to the soul,
are said to be the eyes,
but practice and experience,
can help them tell lies.
Actions, reactions,
rejection and attractions,
cause to concentrate,
and reasons for distractions,
say more about the soul,
than the eyes ever could,
so, when you look at a face,
take in the entire attitude.

08/09/06

Ancestral Intelligence

Ancestral intelligence
is information
passed down,
it's how you wear your history,
with the warmth of a gown,
Awareness of feelings
through the poker
stare,
cutting through the gloom
and dazzling glare,
a small scratch on the
surface through
gentle talk,
can lift someone's shoulders
and straighten
their walk,
but accept their kindness with open
arms,
their well-meaning questions are
sympathetic charms,
- gathered,
the positiveness,
as you go with the flow,
must not be abused for
a mere tell and
show,
such a small word but
profound in effect,
trust is from the heart,
not the intellect,
so, few names yet so many faces,
friends are remembered
in the strangest of
places,
You've met them before in
a down pour,
will they enjoy the gentle rain?
Can I sit in silence without
awkwardness felt,
my fear of over-
confidence is usually
dwelt,
I used to restrain my
happiness now I'm
giving it a push,
but I don't mind it
happening slowly,
I'm not about the rush,
life has more than the
ultimate high,
memories of joy are the
ones that let you fly,
they make you smile
and laugh out loud,
and when told in company,
they lighten the try.

A story here and there
seems to work
fine,
I feel like I've grown up
always gauging attention,
making people happy is my
cure and prevention,
but it's open to attack,
compassion is not easy,
but nice in this world is
usually walked upon,
when will this attitude
see the dawn,
but I'll carry on living,
and carry on giving,
for I feel the life swirling
in my soul.

'06

A thought

I thought I saw a thought,
but it went quickly, and I forgot.
It came again but did not refrain,
its times its own within
this spherical dome,
bouncing around
perpetual thoughts,
no time to wait in parking lots,
there are tracks and traces
and empty places,
forks and junctions
and roundabouts,
all roads taken without any doubts,
all points of the compass,
all are combined,
for that anyone instant,
in anyone's mind.

'07/06

The Beautiful mind

How beautiful the mind is,
to drift along in the expanse,
to gaze in the sunshine,
or a moonlit trance.
Lucid and fluid,
changing with the mood,
unlike the tides of the ocean,
a lunar attraction not
yet understood.
Brightening your day,
like putting solar wind in your sails,
a quiet moment of thought
almost never fails.
An up-lifting thermal
from a synaptic source,
of memories that are married
never to divorce.
It's the only place you can get lost,
and in an instant be back,
So each time you wander,
it's safe to take the least taken track.
With its true capacity unknown,
a mystery to mankind,
never forget the power of
the beautiful mind.

11/11/06

Abounds

My mind abounds,
on the grounds
of a vivid and a wild imagination,
From a one-man army,
loose cannon, lone
gun!

To the charmer of millions,
but the lover of one.
Far-fetched dreams, if
aired for discussion,
but I made pipes to keep them in,
So, tell me, who holds the key?

11/12/06

Advantage

Now that I realize all that I am,
I'm still myself without the calm,
the certainty I had and
always felt before,
returns in waves without the roar,
when my confidence is high,
I tell a story with a tale,
that gives a smile of warmth,
beyond the pale,
I miss that connection,
and I mean no offence,
when I'm quiet and reserved,
just sitting on the fence,
I mean no pretention,
and I feel your unease,
but I feel it too,
so just give me a squeeze,
I want to tell everyone,
my confidence is low,
I don't want to moan,
and create a bad flow,
I wonder if I started
by saying it first,
how many would take advantage,
and drink with a thirst?
It's obvious to all,
so why not create a
common ground?
There's nothing more I enjoy,
than a young confidence found.
It destroys me inside,
to think I'm losing the skill,
of spurring young minds,
to believe in their will,
Where is my passion?
How much can I show?
Does anybody know?

'16

Homeless

Lying in the street with
nothing to eat,
eyes pouring over the rain,
locked up in a shed
without any bed,
tripping on acid,
outta my head,
at first, I faultered,
then I squared,
but the sound that I saw
was something I heard.
Eyes playing tricks,
rats in the mix,
fear and loathing and
lots of foreboding,
awake in the morning,
pain in the heart,
10 quick press-ups,
good for a start,
push the embolism out if
that's how it works,
no-one to help,
we all have our quirks.
Now for day and
somewhere to reside,
I'm not going home because a
mental asylum I can't abide...

01/02/17

Torridness

As I lay,
in torrid dreams,
I felt the grasp,
of the underworld,
it sucked the soul,
my energy of life,
the recurrence of this
phenomena,
as I slept was rife,
this one was bad,
I was about to die,
I woke with a fright,
and rapid intakes of breath,
my heart nearly exploded,
as I faced my death,
I sat up straight,
pulled my back against
the wall,
preparing and waiting,
for the witches' call.

11/11/17

Cliffs no Moher

At the top, looking down,
beware of the frown,
the crease released,
stops the down,
the smash of the crown,
hair follicles drowned,
the claret in abundance,
releases the pain,
the swell from hell,
from days of yore,
the fighting and drinking,
are in Moville's folklore,
Guards at the ready,
out of the ray,
comes vitamin 'D',
lying on the beach,
and swimming in the sea,
float on a boat,
and a castle with a moet,
walls and turrets,
and holes for ferrets,
The Vikings,
the likings,
the beauties abound,
when you fall off this wagon,
hit the ground,
run like the wing,
fly with the earth,
Bored to shit!
What to do?
Put the wingsuit and chute on,
and the Cliffs of Moher are gone!

31/12/17

The Chain

The chain of pain,
The whip from the slip,
Suicides hip when you
in a sectional quip,
Not fun for some when just a joke,
Never when it's serious,
for others, it's delerious,
Not done,
not fun,
no deaths needed,
if people have pain,
well, it's about time we bleed it,
suck it dry,
leave the void full of love,

psycho humour,
or just a rumour,
darkest of the dark,
a guiding light,
haunted houses,
in the dead of night.
Loves lost,
lusts mounted,
if the heads are lost,
how can they be counted?
Decapitation,
precipitation,
face tracked with fears,
all because of arears,
deaths of the past,
insurmountable mountains,
but try hard and train,
and you can break the cast
that's been created.

31/12/17

Insert

Boring life, I don't think so,
Love lets you fly,
wings of joy,
boy o boy,
girl on girl,
Sex on a stick,
flick, flick
orgasmic,
spasmodic,
riveted to the bed,
the feeling of dread,
Can I let a roar?
Oh my God,
Shut that door,
the walls are thin,
rubbers in the bin,

Erase all the worries,
let it escape,
Spatial, sensational,
we need a bigger bed,
the headboards coming off,
the demons are dead.

31/12/17

Line it

Line, line, line,
Time, time, time,
Sublime,
Extreme,
Serene,
bubble,
trouble,
Cough,
trough,
Pig,
Swig.
flow,
bro,
brow,
Cow,
Spoke,
broke,
Smoke,
health,
Wealth,
bequeath,
the wreath.

31/12/17

Mysteries

I said goodbye, and I choke,
write with writh,
Salt in the bath,
Salt in the wounds,
Now feel the wrath,
absurds the word,
the feeling is blurred,
the outcomes oblivion,
Distance prevail,
foreign countries,
Alien lands,
green in colour,
bye gods given hands,
the sea is swimming,
and licks the shores,
the tumble weed burns,
the waves on the floors,
of a beach that was reached,
and love galores.

01/01/18

'69

9 to 6, 6 to 9,
walking and talking,
all of the time,
train time,
bus time,
any time,
Cafes,
Bars,
(The backs of cars),
Loves lusts last far,
jump on join the ride.

01/01/18

All an illusion

Scab,
Slab,
Nabb,
Rab,
hab(s)
Mabs,
Insertion of diversion,
causes of consternation,
ablation,
the movements slow and oblique,
melted,
felt it,
lost marrying a princess,
Spell broken,
She's spoken,
it was an illusion all along,
felt eternity – wasn't my own,
felt all of them connecting,
destiny's a quest,
behest,
the lest,
you're meeting the best,
Now for a queen and life serene.

01/01/18

O'Douls

Distant shores,
Women of pores,
Sweat, flipping, blinding,
horned to the cores,
bull by the horns,
horns by the bull,
drink my full,
until you come,
respected, elected, reflected,

elated, deflated, castrated,
balls returned,
carpe diem,
Steal a kiss,
eternal bliss,
drink the piss,
mine's O'Douls,
The magnitudes are drooling,
We're turning into ghouls,
Let flight,
outta sight,
bouncing with height,
can we take it?
We've been designed for the right.

'01/18

Palates

Plates are empty,
fork prongs are bent,
eyeballs on the wall,
energy is spent,
hanging like conkers,
God, I need a doll,
dancing with Lunasa,
Moon on the fall,
Sunshine is terrible,
it gets in my eyes,
desert storm,
we do all despise.

02/01/18

They're out to Annoy

Out to annoy,
Out to rule,
Resilience prevails,
Who looks the fool?
Right foot feels the soul,

Tip-toeing in reverse,
Everything they are doing,
Is fucking perverse,
Sadness prevails,
When I think of the past,
Gun to the head,
Give it a blast,
Kurt Cobain I feel your pain,
Ronny Drew, I feel the strain,
Guinness for breakfast,
Buckfast for lunch,
Letterkenny General,
thanks a bunch!

02/01/18

Shitzo Diverse

The universe is dividing,
all for one dual compatibility,
come out fighting your 30 now,
Mc Gregor doesn't stand a chance!
Did that tune,
then ultra oligarchy fulfill the plot,
It's ending with love
black eyes the lot,
Love is strained,
Love is a plot,
Why so tenses,
There's tea in the pot,
Love in the thirties,
Smells gal lour,
Tracy wtf,
Pig swill me hole,
There's gas in the street,
Where two heads meet,
Ultra oligarchy, I will rule it,
Hands shot guided created,
From unbeknownst to where,
He could write from now
until Christmas,

You hear our thoughts,
Ogden away,
The door slams shut.

02/01/18

There are rumours these poems were written while drunk!

Your Pie Hole

Pestilence, bitterness, of
course, it went in,
The thoughts of being a no-one,
Is where to begin,
Benign it's a Scara Manga,
A history of violence oh
no, I mean aggression,
Who the fuck doesn't,
Welcome to the Fleadh Coel,
I love the Irish,
I love being me,
It's the others, or am I paranoid,
No their afraid to be free,
He faltered,
he's played,
There loving / stealing his humour,
Your are on TV,
Oh Wahoo wahee,
Whaoooh.

02/01/18

Leg Before Wicket

LGBT,
LBW,
Whets that you C,
Fuck me in the temple,
Fuck me in the street,
When two Thrans meet,
Writings getting bigger,
Energy has gone from the hand,
Solely left balls in a bind,
Shadow has gone from the eye,
Spirit from the left,
Provosted on the right,
Finger and thumb,
Press up begin,
Welcome to the Oligarchs,
What's there was there before,
I reiterate (It's just ahh
you did see it!),
I'm putting charts,
Never pitt bruvers,
Yap does it again,
It's not his word,
That's why they refrain,
They took the pride out,
Because I failed not to sin,
He's speaking, I put conjuring,
Through the devil/Lord,
It's mixed in begin,
Welcome to Genius,
Everyone's on the level,
There's eyes fucking everywhere,
Thrown in Cork,
Unveiled in the street,
Brides at the door come in come in,
Writing everywhere,
It's a catharsis of power,
Frenzy of evidence,
Silver screen learning,
Oh know he knowth too much,
Good book has taken off him,
Welcome to France,
Where did he get the head,
I would not let them in on it,
Not one bloody sinner,
Who'd go near that
working class Heron,

Learn the guitar,
Bird cages ready welcome
to Saint Martin,
He threatened my son, no,
you treat him well,
You keep on writing
the giants of fell,
Fall upon my shoulder,
Fall on my Knife,
Ni neirt go cur le cheile,
Piss taking, we will see.

02/01/18

Flute

Her heart haith fluttered,
Digging the heel,
Well healed he felt,
An ode to P.Cuffy,
You're current, you're collected,
You're lifted and laid,
Is it any wonder you feel guilty
your constantly splayed,
Welcome to bachelorhood,
Your forty years ago,
The ceasefire is current,
Welcome to the BBC, the
worlds about to blow,
James Blunt surfaced again,
They don't want me to have fame,
Enough,
Hon nuit,
Moneys Money Love is life,
I am a physic, and I'm okay,
Because I talk to boys,
they think I'm gay,
I'm a woman and that's alright.
He must have some money,
That man wrote Flight,
Young Juans, the man
he wrote Em&Em,
Everyone's tuning in I
see them connecting,
Every thought and every squint,
Is noted,
Doted,
Then torn apart,
Then your brain is
driving them insane.

02/01/18

Fubar

Fucked up fubared beyond control,
Resilience is paramount,
This town is in a hole,
Party animal central,
The naughtiest are gone,
We are in our teens,
People moving away,
they are busting their spleens,
We are the God damn Spartans,
I trained in Sparta,
What's the matta?
You're on the mat.

28/01/18

Innit

Abandon sleep,
In snooze, not a peep,
In silence, we weep,
In life,
In love,
In the relax,
In the peace,
In the woods,

In the Gladiators,
In the womb,
In the love,
In the tomb.

28/01/18

The lost poem

It was enmass,
it was a day,
When all at play,
I've has(ssle) it,
The poem somewhere,
the love of the mass,
peace it be,
let love free,
be @ one,
within the net,
fish that flee,
escape the fret.

03/02/18

Solace

Spaltering about,
thoughts in the bin,
is it peace,
or is it a sin?
It's some sort of solace,
if not good,
the hang-overs are brutal,
negligible,
it's pew,
it's a solaced life,
and a cultured wife,
where is my soul?
Beleaguered in pole,
pos-,

I felt it sucked dry,
to my very last breath,
but ignorance took over,
and the disease almost left,
I looked out the window,
into the night's sky,
determined to live,
and never to die.

02/03/18

Precise

Sex sex sex!
Stories no gories,
tiresome fight,
about not being,
allowed to take flight,
crowned from above,
Stability in the dove,
strap on the wings,
give them some love,
piece of pie,
personality arises,
Central nervous system,
Shudders when I cum,
Snowball chance in a swell,
that I'll ever lie down,
when the love that is coming,
as I ascend from Hell,
and don my gown.

19/03/18

Shoulders for boulders

The games we play,
with heads that stay,
firmly upon our shoulders,
Boulders lifted,

lives that have shifted,
different roots,
with marching boots,
Steading hitting the mac,
thump, thump, thump,
jump, jump, jump,
over the hurdles of years,
tears overlaid fears,
thanks to pranks and spanks,
I created ranks
LIKE tanks.

19/03/18

Christmas

T'is the season,
to be jolly,
fun-filled festivities,
jovial jawbreakers,
That kin,
would win,
if the filter wasn't broken,
the neurons flashing,
Brains alive,
the dice are in a hive,
roll them carefree,
and you'll get double 6,
if this was Christmas.

26/03/18

Fire

Karate is in my blood and
so now are the sausages,
burnt to a crisp,
slash they're Godam fucking tasty,
The Jameson's good,
but I needed the food,
it wouldn't be a BBQ without it,
Eyes adjusting, fire musting,
flames are nearly out,
sticks are gone,
but I'm still Juan,
so, there's nothing to
fucking worry about,
I emanate heat.

27/03/18

Yoga

Mediate, meditate,
let the flow go,
forgo the blow,
that downs your sails,
Inhales, exhales,
beyond the pales,
Chillax, relax,
Chill the bod,
let the mind race,
then reign in the pace,
rip off the face,
that's non-committal
to grace,
reprieve, deceive,
the thoughts that grieve,
abound tied tight,
is the pain, that is slight?
Niggling, purging,
wearing it down,
dig out the roots,
that are too big
for their boots,
let them walk,
the plank feels the
strain,
as they come of
edge,

their obedience will pledge,
a wonderous and fruitful new beginning,
pick a circle of sharks,
for those little quarks,
let them flutter in the ethereal wind,
out with the net,
gather them when they've met,
and let them sink or swim.
Namaste.

27/03/18

My Yoga teacher asked me to pen a poem for her. This is the result ;)

Yoga for Celine

Yoga's a mind,
@ peace with the soul,
When you're limber, supple
and end up on the pole,
you'll flex your pecs,
and carry life's toll,
You'll leave the crowds,
of passers-by,
forget about the whiskey,
forget about the rye,
dry the eye,
and learn not to cry,
breathe with life,
not let it get you down,
and clear the wrinkle,
that caused the frown,
You'll stretch the strands
and fibre of your being,
into the flax of the sounds,
without you seeing,
You'll feel the air,
within your mind,
travel through your body,
and give you that extra inch,
that might get you out of a bind.
The love that's bestowed,
is from Celine and her Zen,
it effects my body,
and comes out through my pen!
The zenith,
I penith,
and free up some space
and take my place,
in the human race.

18/07/18

Life not simple

Dinner in the hospital,
Shards in the dark,
Walking around town,
waiting for the spark,
all in the mind,
tension disappeared,
all thoughts are irrelevant,
the terrorisms speared,
finding my place,
in the Irish race,
drinking's a culture,
one I disbanded,
and found my way in,
a Jamie with water,
is hardly a sin,
calories negligible,
social galore,
cut me I'm bleeding,
open a pore,
sperm tastes of apples,

so she said,
play on the cider,
every woman I see,
I want to ride her.

02/09/18

Irma

Words fly off the page,
That was bugs welcome
to the spark,
That's mammy outside,
Oh wait, it's not,
Dark and dusky morning on
a plane bound for nowhere,
Crosshair,
I am down with,
You're ready,
Take the fucking,
Reep what you sow,
In an ellocuint fashion,
A sword for a nife,
Who needs the "Kay",
Weetabix is tasty,
Words are at play,
The poet named Wordworth,
Alota money,
Lears,
Fucking clueless,
Bound tight lyin in the dirt
(party like the Irish? I know
what you did you cants!),
Gets up and starts walking. Does
he has no memory of the plot?
Well, yes, he does,
Welcome to memorandum.

02/09/18

Jesus wept

I'm a poet, yeah, why you?
Got a problem with that?
Jesus wept!
Love in a puddle,
total avoidance,
they all can scram,
the love in a bucket,
welcome to Nantucket,
whale blubber my hole,
that fucker is heavyweight,
me balls he opinions galore,
that guy fucked you,
he's her fucked senseless,
Shoa moans mutha fucka.

02/09/18

DJ

Joyce country, gay in a band,
You'll get no peace and that's,
(eyes directed towards the
cup (lyons tea)) from,
a lion. Why what he stills,
hold grudges,
meet & fear,
Nat one welcome to the fingers,
clasp I love you,
you put fear in Juan,
love life and fruit of
the loom whom,
hierarchy, just love life.

02/09/18

Eastumour

Tumour (Easter) this
fucker is loaded,
slow down you're going too fast,
Has he got a woman?
Benign belay be writing
what we day,
Interrupt flow freely no
commas or stops,
It has an effect, have
they lost the plot?
This shit is genius, it's exactly
what they have done,
All involved dont want to hear,
It's all pure lunacy,
Who the fucking man,
Is he to get mercy?
A beat you to the punch,
haha nah nah,
He hears he feels,
uniform is needed,
GAA lower,
Foclair Humpty Dumpty,
Well, he has put himself
back together,
Heirplay,
Fucked up fubared
beyond recognition,
Lift him commas are coming,
Love lift fear behoven,
Feared unbehoven,
Internet in the brain,
You just got your knee back,
Burned in feel the heat,
Cross to bear,
Weird at the black cross in the air,
If this is scitzo?
Then, Im all for it,
Nambi pambi,
smoke in the air,
The writing is senseiful,
Booze hounds will get it,
Piece in the membrane,
Welcome to genetitist,
This is crappola,
Whose the judge
Welcome to Niall,
Too old for styling,
Welcome to Johna,
Ya good thing ya,
Out and about having fun,
Tinkers in town,
They're already here.

02/09/18

U

They're watching they love you,
Smoke veils and threats,
Testing, testing one
two,
Wan two,
Juan can sing YOUR HEARTS,
OUT TO THE GLORY OF THE
MAN RABBIE WILLIAMS,
ya man, of course, ye can,
Orlath, I love you,
Dan anthracite,
Dust mortimer, don't fart.

02/09/18

Welcome

Keep on writing. Welcome to DaWett,
that's from Dan,
take him for a beer,
that kid needs a break,
yeah, you,
I can see it in his eyes,
deathly silent rigormortis
(Dayworker! ☺),
rigid solid,
No rest for the wicked,
paper is scare..sce.

02/09/18

Sprinkle

Start it with moet,
A sparkle to the day,
drunk or not,
the mamosa was gorgeous,
have you lost the plot?
you see it on both sides,
you're mentally aware,
ah, hair ah care,
subjew down trodden,
mentally off track,
and he's back,
it's galloping in,
Juan's giving it power.
you are in fucking grey skill,
Upper L.a,
East side west side,
They all tuning,
he's getting his nutts squeezed,
Ephemeral thought,
Dust in the wind,
that's what they had planned,
the whole lots in the bin.

13/09/18

Psalm

"Lord, teach us how short life is,
that we may become wise!"
Psalm: Anonymous

23/10/18

Gib

On the rock,
thinking like Spock,
how the hell do I get out of here?
The spear of destiny,
is wavering out of control,
late night bars,
and back on the Dole,
it nearly worked out,
the states were in sight,
the Superyacht life,
was to be fly by night,
L.A dreams,
were to be realised,
a lift on a yacht,
that has been despised,
digs here,
digs there,
if you don't fuck off,
it's me you will fear,
it's my life,
it's my career,
why fuck it up on me?
When I'm trying to be sincere.

23/10/18

Letterkenny

Scare you,
scare me,
ho ho,
he he
simpleton,
dunce,
all from runts,
who gives them the fucking power,
to behave like cunts,
accosted in the street,
everyone has an opinion,
do they not realize,
I do Rilion,
if they keep it up,
my tongue will lash,
and not your back,
your head will smash.

23/10/18

Sun in the sky with dreams

Sun in the sky,
lets my wings fly,
the scent in the air,
makes me shave my hair,
Clean cut,
Shaved to the bone,
tax worked out,
I'll be no Al Capone,
maybe in nature,
but not in the clink,
Some men are an Island,
I'll live on my own,
and I will not sink,
I'll fill it with mo cairde,
We'll have craic and fun,
So long despair,
and when Metaphysically
wrinkle-free,
Cleanse, Synthesize and clear,
every thought you so badly hold,
for a killing spree,
You want to let go the bad,
and hold on to the good,
So let go the suppression,
and take off the hood.

23/10/18

Antibes

Love in the sun,
Summer has begun,
Fun, frolics,
and a tight little bum,
muscles galore,
head straight and square,
now for a job,
and so long despair!

11/07/18

Dole day

A drunken day,
where Fanjita will pay,
for all her cigarettes
and wine,
And Leeroy will pimp,
Fanjita to squeal,
and have all his minions to
heel,
he will give out his playboy
for them to pine,
a dole day to remember,

it was one of a kind,
it was alphoid, to begin with,
but it turned out benign,
the betazoid attachment,
drained the life and
soul from my mind,
sucked out all my blood,
downed my class,
and took the town
up her scrawny ass,
t'was bright and sunny,
as we stood in the queue,
all the hoods were there,
and they did not care!

11/07/18

Stuck

Stuck in the corner,
all alone in the dark,
Confidence stricken,
by the littlest quark,
energy flowing,
in and out,
Surveillance moving,
waiting for the spark.

01/12/18

Bridges and fridges

Bridges and fridges,
I've been Ironweed,
there's no wavering decision,
I've comma far,
to go back now,
ladies of the night,
they are prescription drugs,
they should be prescribed
to everyone,
including the girls,
We'll blast out the music,
give them the whirls,
and we'll ship Champagne
in the suds.

01/12/18

Coerced

Locked in a cauldron,
witches abound,
flaring green eyes,
and fire on the ground,
smoke fills the air,
all around me is war,
everything I think
of,
is beware, beware,
the thoughts are created,
in my mind's eye,
translucent in nature,
they let my mind fly,
the thoughts are coercive,
they're in earshot and thought,
when I think of a sentence,
they've already got,
when the public is around,
my thoughts are answered
with a nod,
the cars have a voice,
the intent speaks.

18/10/19

A hundred years have come and gone

A hundred beers have
come and gone,
I look at the moon before the dawn,
I wonder at the magnitude,
Of another being,
Sitting up there without me seeing,
Lazing in the dust,
As it's about to settle,
A heart full of love,
And a conscience of metal,
Loves lost,
Love will win,
We are the young breed
that always wins,
We win in our hearts,
We win in our minds,
The daily chore of life,
Are not in our grinds,
We haven't studied,
For what is to come,
The destiny they planned is
about to come undone,
They write me off,
Who are they to plan,
They haven't met a Shroove
man who is more than thran,
We win in our hearts,
We win in our minds,
They are not the ones,
Who draw the blinds,
I did drugs,
It's not me,
But the apparitions I now live with,
Have joined the melee,
They live with me constantly,
From days of yore,
I love the ancestral intelligence,
I want to hear more,
They talk to me constantly,
Narrating my thoughts,
What is the outcome,
For that, they're drawing lots?

'06/19 & '01/21

Axe no questions. Tell no lies

The politics of power,
have always caught my eye,
from the schoolyard as a kid,
to watching grown men lie.
The moment it was defined for me,
what politics really was,
the belief in a change for the better,
caused a stirring in my clause.
The purple shroud of mystery,
that's worn with so much pride,
is just a scam to block the damn,
so every lamb can hide.
Out in the open,
where we all can see,
is where they stand upon the tree,
branches supporting,
to the roots in the ground,
how long will they stand there?
When the axe is found?
Chipping away with every mistake,
We'll whip up the wind that'll
make the bow break.
It's the safety net then,
that's formed through
their opinion,
deciding if their fate,
feels like a minion.

Correctness or not,
conversations are forgotten,
but insults intended,
fester until they're rotten,
but only if you let them,
and I wouldn't bet on them,
deceived is to be believed,
in their follower's party
pick on the loner,
then laugh at him heartily,
everyone leads,
they're all at the back,
no-one at the front,
they're all screaming attack,
the passion and wealth,
and no bloody stealth,
no training,
all feigning,
staggered Jesus's,
reigning,
squashed and moshed,
their trundled hopes joshed,
by parties greater,
and out of the dome,
the little squirrels that naw,
in the damned of their town,
they won't stop it,
'til they cop it,
they want everyone down,
not only to their level,
but below the floorboards,
buried in a soul,
of a bastard's putrid holes,
just like theirs,
the strong of us taking the toll,
they sit back,

armchair rebels,
taxi driver mirror practicing,
for when they meet the real deal,
and show how they feel,
Ooohh, I'm so scared,
You fuck wits are nasty,
In numbers, you're strong,
All trying to be Rasty,
Smoking the weed,
A whole town on one man,
Oh, you are all so brave,
Well, watch me fuck you'all up
when I behave the knave,
Excited,
Delighted,
I will be,
To pull down your
Erigal Letterkenny,
And sell your scree,
The japs will love it,
You can sycophantically
suck their eye,
And when I leave town,
You all can carry on playing I-spy,
incestuous ideas and behaviour,
of an insular fold,
festering flies,
as in the market place they dwell,
(Nietszche had it right!!!!!),
the faithful fabric of society,
they are about to fell,
they know no better,
from their intellect,
With them in charge,
the world would be wrecked!

ST. PAT'S MENTAL ASYLUM DUBLIN

02/07/03

If dreams could come true

If dreams could come true,
What would we do?
Would mine affect yours?
then we'd all be in the sewers,
Forget all that shit,
We can dream it'll never happen,
Non-conflicting dreams,
that'll leave God flapping!!
The devil will dance,
in the heart of the earth,
he'll throw his fork
over his shoulder,
and off he'll prance,
More fuel for the fire,
like a burning black tyre,
But it's not for dreamers,
as you might suspect,
It's for the shrimp on the barbie,
and the sweet devils dialect,
Oh, what a party!!!,
We're going to have,
for the beer competitions,
We'll split the teams in half!!
My God! Said a man,
"if anyone can, lucifer,
you certainly can",
Gods here too?
What do you mean?
This is blasphemous,
it's downright obscene,
you're onto this together?
Said the nosey old guy,
Fuck off, said God,
While I finish my rye!
With a slurp & sup,
and with one swift hand,
he crushed the cup!
He turned to the guy,
and said to him,
"It's all a game,
don't you see?"
Just keep your eye on
the scoreboard,
Or you'll be closer
to ME!

'03

I'm.....

I'm a wanderer,
I'm a ponderer,
I'm a loner,
I'm a moaner,
I'm a suggestor,
I'm a molester,
I'm a joker,
I'm a stoker,
I'm a broker,
I'm a choke choker,
I'm an mooner,
I'm a crooner,
I'm a fighter,
I'm a writer,
I'm a lover,
I'm a cover,
I'm a shielder,
I'm a yielder,
I'm a counter puncher,
I'm a mounter,
I'm a canter,
I'm a ranter,
I'm a raver,
I'm a paver.

09/07/03

Depression

Are you deflated?
Down in the dumps?
Hurry up people....
Where are the pumps?
I'm sinking quite fast,
and I need some air,
Where are the people,
Who said they care?
Ah, here she comes,
my lovely wife,
She'll understand me,
and give breath to my life.
Why does it always rain on me?
I'm unhappy enough,
Can't you see?
But I will see clearly,
when the rain has gone,
18 years is a while,
but it's not a lifetime long.
It'll pass in a while,
Chin up and be strong,
however it's instigated,
look it straight in the eye,
from now and in the future,
Till the day you
DIE!

10/07/03 & '04/21

War and Peace

Churchill said,
"War is only just,
when all other means of peace
has been exhausted."
So, pick your political target,
and shoot it or blast it.
Not like the Americans,
who use collateral damage,
by bombing schools and hospitals,
creating colossal carnage.
What's their agenda?
Is it war and peace?
Or a piece of war?
They enjoy the power rush,
like driving a muscle car,
overwhelmed and inebriated,
by the exuberance of
their own verbosity.
They plunder and pillage,
all non-American cities,
countries a far from their
own lovely land,
and the only disaster's they receive,
is by the act of Gods hand,
the weather,
two buildings are flattened,
to ground zero,
and the fucking yanks,
think George Dubya a hero?
His tyranny had to be stopped,
American hearts opened,
I believe in no borders at all,
Pride in a country,
Makes men fall,
Let them see the truth
of war for wealth,
Of how their leaders use disguise,
Plausible deniability,
AND lies, lies, LIES!!!
Let's see what the world thinks,
when their true intentions
are shown,
When their thoughts of
world domination,
are fully grown,

the spoils of war,
and roads of tar,
oil for your car,
and talk about it in a bar,
But the world won't let him,
we'll stand tall and be counted,
no prouder people there
are on this earth,
we'll smile at the
grandiose delusions.
But we'll hide our mirth,
I don't believe in war,
But I do like fighting,
Everybody's a warrior at heart,
It comes natural to us humans,
so, we'll hit the same spot TWICE,
With a single bolt of lightning!
So, come on, Mr. Presidente,
bring it on,
send your best,
I'll take them on!
I'm from Donegal & Derry,
AND my name is Juan.

11/07/03

Nothing

If you weren't mad
before you came in,
it'll slowly ambush you,
the longer you stay,
the price is freedom and boredom,
and you'll certainly pay!
No stimulus only the nurses,
there's nothing to do,
and eventually they just say,
fuck you,
I see they get pissed off as well,
but they can go home,

we're left irritated and
frustrated as hell,
with all the cameras,
and the constant eyes and ears,
the constant attention is
to allay their fears.
It's like big brother,
without the votes and
money and the end,
but it's their reputation,
they have to defend.
What drugs are you on?
Oh, that's a colourful blend!
Has it made a difference?
Well, neither to me!
It feels like jail,
where one and all are guilty free!
So, we'll go with the program
and suck it and see!

14/07/03

I wrote this to get out of St. Pat's.

Truth

Well, doctor Slim,
it's been a blast,
I've made a lot of new friends,
and they're not in the past,
between the patients and the staff,
We've laughed,
at first, I didn't understand,
the blatant reticence,
and your reluctance to move me,
but now it makes sense,
the drugs do work,
not like the song said,
and the lack of activity,
made room for my bed,

I've slept the sleep,
of a thousand dreams,
yet I did not die,
or wake up with screams,
so, I take back what I said,
Both to your face,
and behind your back,
it wasn't all that bad,
just that your visiting was slack!
But you're busy people,
and this I comprehend,
and I now firmly believe,
You've all been a God
SEND!!!

14/07/03

University of life

So, now I start from the
beginning of the page,
No hands of anger,
or inner rage,
Not a child's delight,
to see a fight,
if only the words of jest,
if they do it once,
then do it lest.
As for now and in the future,
cage of rage,
is closed wide shut,
But it was all a stage,
and boy could we perform,
My best education,
of how to be norm.
I thank my parents,
for what I've got,
and not jealous,
for what I've not.
If or is,
GODS will or not,
- I read a bit a bible and
oh my god,
I nearly become a disciple,
I took a double take,
- what's that you say?
Doesn't GOD make a mistake?
I believe this true,
but what am I to do,
- I look and walk & talk like you?
We run gods course,
of a little remorse,
And when we look
guilt free enough,
you're outta the rough,
rolling away on the lovely fairway.
So, mistake I think not,
But that's not our lot.
So, take it as it comes,
- you may not like it,
but acceptance will make
you feel like you had it,
Begrudge no man,
who has made himself
by his own hand,
for he is the Man who can carry
the world upon his shoulders,
and laugh and luck at life,
through the eyes of a child,
he will be the Man who
put the letters
'L'I'M'D' in mild,
So, continue the tail,
when in circles for a minute.
The university of life,
taught by daddy,mammy,
and the ducklings.

15/07/03

Crystal clear

Is it four walls,
or an opaque fence?
That frustrates the mind
and leaves out common sense?
They tell me it's freedom
but I don't believe'um.
There's fuck all to do,
but visitors are comin,
so, I must stay here!
Where the hell are they?
What's keeping them?
Stuck in traffic?
Stuck in a metal hem?
Hemmed in by cars,
and no way out,
I can sympathize with them,
it makes me scream and shout,
So, let me FUCKING OUT!
I'm pissed off acting sad,
to make them all feel glad,
their diagnosis was right,
when really all I am doing
is fooling them,
knowing it's all a load of shite,
my mind is clear,
as crystal as can be,
but only a select few see it,
and one of them is me.

16/07/03

Patience

Patience is a virtue,
but mines are restrained
by a curfew.
There must be some in there,
it's not like I don't care,
Just sometimes I don't show it,
but surely you know it.
When I talk to children,
or the elderly & old,
I'm like magma or lava,
I'm cool but not cold,
The patience will show,
and those who I mention,
Certainly know,
I've no time for people,
who forget their inner child,
they forget how to live,
and go a little wild,
a life full of boredom,
they are destined to lead,
It's the fruit of life,
they badly need,
Vitamin D from their
inner light,
the shine that burns,
within their soul,
So, don't dampen or darken,
Your ambition or goal,
live life to the max
and till you've got it,
don't relax,
Then enjoy the fun,
in the summer
SUN!

20/07/03

Written for Flo

Together

If like they say,
what's for you,
won't go by you,
Then there's no need
for me to feel blue,
I think of you when we are apart,
even though our journey's
just beginning,
we haven't even passed start!
I follow my heart,
but I have faith in my mind,
God must be missing an angel,
maybe he sent you to me,
as a gift of a kind?
I enjoy the talk,
and when we walk the walk,
I like your confidence,
and sure footed approach,
your feelings for me,
no-one could reproach,
so, follow your heart,
and lead with your mind,
and tell all the doubters,
you've met one of a KIND!!!

26/07/03

Crosswords

Crosswords can often
be a crossroads,
you've to look at the words,
and decide the mode,
your train of thought,
the path to take,
if you think you're right,
and write it in,
and then you're wrong,
well, then you're caught!
So, I suggest you use a pencil,
and when using a pen,
keep it neat,
so, use a stencil!
Cos if you want the money,
they've to be able to read it.
And if there's enough of a prize,
you can visit somewhere sunny,
so, before you send it in,
make sure it's right, and
the words are neat,
then you'll be put in the draw,
with a chance to win.

27/07/03

Biomedical material

Should it be there,
or should it not?
Definitely without it,
you would be caught!
Just cos you use it,
it doesn't say who you are,
it's not material,
like a Jaguar,
You may need it from birth,
but that can't be helped,
it all began when as an embryo,
and now the material you need,
it necessarily bio,
but it'll keep you from pain,
and hopefully sane,
Out of trouble and strife,
and give you a good aul
LIFE!

Childs play

'03

One flew into the cuckoo next,
looking for guidance,
and a well-earned rest.
The resultant reception,
was a rather mixed bag,
most of the cool nurses were there,
but there still remains
the odd toe-rag,
rules have been added,
subtracted and doubled,
so, it's understandable to see,
why we are all so troubled,
it's like playing football
with a friend,
who keeps moving the post,
demoralizing our spirits,
'til all you are left with
are the ghosts,
but in the true fighting
IRISH style,
we show our true IRISH form,
rise above all bureaucracy,
and sail through the storm,
we're not the untouchables,
that's why we were forced to
come here for your help,
and if we step out of line,
you better not give us a skelp,
but a bit of common sense,
should be the prevailing wind,
not a stereotypical view,
that we all have sinned,
this is directed,
at only one or two,
so, thanks and God bless to y'all,
I must go back,
from where I flew.

A song for paradise

27/07/03

Rhapsody's a word,
I'm not sure on the specifics,
but I think it's a song,
If I had a dictionary,
I'd give you the exact
meaning of wanking,
but what I do know is this,
that within your body,
it can cause a wonderful feeling,
with the vibes and the beats,
the sense of rhythm and bass,,
I think it's a disgrace,
It can cause such happiness,
Exhilarating joy,
If sung or played properly,
by the correct girl or boy,
The lyrics are paramount,
Cos, they make the tune,
without them, they'd be lost,
like a way ward ballon
But if you play it right,
what exquisite delight,
from the heaving mass
of the crowd,
who for more shout out loud,
so, if you want the feeling,
to make you happy,
open your ears for a
helluva Rhapsody!

27/07/03

The Ums

This is all about life in Donegal,
Where we hate all be grudgers,
and say fuck'em all,
We live life to the fullest,
we like a life full of fun,
we work hard and play hard,
as 4 those who don't,
they can stick it up their bums,
Cos our motto's pretty cool,
it's not about the 'UMS,
There's the first one listed,
and you show it with your thumb,
we live life to the fullest,
so that is MAXIM'UM,
you show the second
with your index,
and take down your thumb,
this one's for empty glasses,
so, it's a MINIM'UM,
and last but not least,
so, bang it on your drum,
take down your index,
extend your middle finger,
and just say,
FUCK'UM!

28/07/03

Written for Nurse Monica who would never carry a lighter in the ICU where you couldn't have your own.

Monica

Hey Monica,
you're like a harmonica,
you bring music to my ears.
The only problem is it
makes them bleed,
I didn't expect you to
look at my poem,
cos you probably can't even read.
I'd say you're lucky,
I'm not a spontaneous fighter,
It doesn't surprise me,
you don't carry a lighter.
But if you continue as you are,
your life will rise in flames,
but fuck you,
what odds is it to me,
It's all the same,
as they say at home,
you won't see it from my house!
But there's no need to look,
or talk down to people,
like they're a louse,
It's easier to be nice,
than it is to be not,
I believe you treat
everyone with respect,
I don't expect a lot.
But it's your life, so fuck you,
And if you stay on that path,
It'll turn into POO!!!

28/07/03

The Galway races

To ride and run,
in the summer sun,
but it's Ireland,
so, it's probably rain.
So, it's straight to the bar,
to watch from afar,
they're beautiful,
in every single way,
and that's the woman,
with their hats,
and of course, the horses
eating their hay,
when they run,
after their vegetarian meal,
their skirts are blown,
up around their necks,
but all that is exposed,
is their dental floss panties,
covering their lovely bums,
after 7 days running,
trying to keep on the
right side of the track,
the woman is tired of trying to
find a rich man who is slack!
From what I hear,
there could also be horses involved,
and that they eat the slow
ones at the end of the race.
If a caveman was watching,
would he just wonder how
much we'd evolved?

28/07/03

Kindred Spirits

Mentally ill,
Oh, what a thrill,
to meet so many people,
outside of Donegal,
who also believe in saying,
to all the conformist - fuck'em all,
It's a nice place to be but
only for a while,
a short stay – a visit,
is more my style,
I firmly believe,
as Patch Adams stated,
Reduce the drugs,
and use laughter to compensate it!
What harm can it do?
But bring happiness and joy,
why not have a video,
a few comedies,
Do we each get a gameboy?
A pack of cards,
or some board games,
to promote interaction,
get people to mix,
and give them a distraction,
cos it's a long enough day,
watching all the free
fucking channels,
why not get paramount,
and the proper MTV?
C'mon, you cunts,
Cough up & pay!!!

28/07/03

A busy day

A busy day,
but it's home time soon,
hip-hip hooray,
No time to even bless myself,
let alone think or drink,
Even when I'm thirsty,
I forget to wink,
but 15 minutes and counting,
I'll be in the pub,
and it'll be drinking I'm after,
not the grub!
Let's hope tomorrow
will soon be over,
Cos I'm planning on beer,
and a massive hangover,
I'm long on patients,
but the staff are short
on their temper,
they like fucking me around,
just for fun,
And it leaves me drinking,
like a dog with distemper,
But busy is good,
It passes the time,
it feels @ the end of the day,
you deserve the wine,
But I enjoy the wank,
it gives me a thrill,
to mix with the Geniuses,
and the Mentally
ILL!!!

29/07/03

Just one minute

I hear a voice in the morning,
and the evening,
the radio and the CD's make
me feel sane again.
But if I tell the doctors
and the nurses,
they'll drug me up for absurdity,
so, I should have been home,
yesterday, yesterday,
Irish homes,
take me home,
to the place where I BELONG,
East Donegal, mountain mama,
Errigals own,
Irish roads, take me home.
The majority of them are nice,
but as the saying goes,
it only takes one bad apple to spoil
what once was a delicious slice.
But don't be impatient,
in fact I know I am,
but they're so fucking slow,
cos if they were in the race,
with the turtle and the hair,
they'd never win it,
cos everything you ask for,
is in a minute.
God forbid they say 5,
cos then you're truly fucked,
one takes an hour,
so, 5 will be next week,
and probably by then,
you'll be dead or very weak!

'03

Just the one

The clouds were spilling rain,
I'd gone for a pint,
and had ten again,
when I had the first one,
it started to fizzle,
Sure, I thought to myself,
I'll wait till it stops,
fire us up another one there,
I can smell those hops,
4,5 and 6,
it was raining bricks,
I said to the barman,
that looks heavy,
I'm not going out in that,
this'll be my lucky 7th bevvy,
I drank number 8,
as quick as I could,
cos I could see it in the barman,
he was in the closing mood,
so, 9 and 10,
I ordered together,
I'll drink them and be happy,
whatever the weather.

30/07/03

I don't love Lucky

Fuck him left, fuck him right,
fuck him sideways,
the fucking bender,
he won't be so smart,
when I put him in a blender.
I thought to be a shrink,
you had to be bright,
but from what I can see,
he needs two arseholes,
to get rid of all his shite.
He'll rue the day,
he ever lied to me,
I'll fuck him up good,
just watch and see.
Spoke to like a child,
He enjoys the patronize,
Well, just watch him tremble,
as I cut him down to size.
I know farmers at home,
who'd keep him for his shite,
he speaks it from both ends,
day and night,
he should start a workshop,
teaching the art of manure,
it's a viral condition,
therefore no cure.
No eye to eye contact,
therefore shifty and sly,
well fuck you, Lucky,
here's your job,
kiss it
GOODBYE!

31/07/03

Fitness

Eat well,
drink well,
everything in moderation.
If you're not fit playing sports,
it can be a hard auld station.
Preoccupation can often be a fault,
some people lock themselves away,
as if in a vault.
You could call it determination,
but with fitness and happiness,
there's sometimes no relation,

train hard, play hard,
is the order of the day,
but don't train at all,
and you'll certainly pay,
So, do a bit of both,
to promote muscle growth,
a fit body means a fit mind,
but slouch around,
and pull your wire,
you'll definitely go blind,
so, get off your ass
stop flicking that bean,
don't be so fucking lazy,
if you do nothing at all
that can be seen,
you'll go fucking crazy.

31/07/03

I asked Nurse Nicola could I make a call on the wall phone for the patients? She said yes and asked me for the number. As I watched, upside down, she keyed in the code to get the outside line on her desk phone. She then transferred it to the wall phone when it answered. I wondered to myself would the code for the outside line work straight off on the wall phone for the patients. I tried it and it did! I told a few other patients I thought I could trust but the knowledge got out to one of the edjits in there and she was caught keying it in, in front of Nicola. We all started laughing at Nicola getting angry at us all making calls without her permission. She got so angry that she ripped the wall phone for us off the wall and screamed that now no-one will make calls!!!

Give us a few seconds

I've something to ask ya -,
have you got time Nicola -,
"Just a minute?" said she,
I'll be with you in a seconda - ",
I know it'll be a little longer,
but the spasm won't kill ya,
They'll make you stronger,
if you're waiting for a light -,
you might have to wait
a few seconds,
that'll take the whole
fucking night -,
the phone lines are down,
depressed as can be -,
what do you expect ripping
it off the wall Nicola?
A shift in power,
she wants it all you see -,
I cracked the codes,
and it's pissed off time for her -,
So, she ripped the phone
off so quick,
it looked like a blur -,
but if I asked her a question,
for a soothing light -,
so, she slowed like a sloth,
not much to my delight -,
Cos I've no phone,
Nor any fucking light!

31/07/03

Sown

I'm a schitzophrenic,
me too!
Now were both stuck in here,
what do we do?
What the movies portray,
is totally wrong,
If it was entered in the oscars,
they'd receive a gong.
It's hard to explain,
but we're actually sane,
we know what we can do,
without restriction.
It's just sometimes we've
got a problem,
between reality and fiction.
But we're not worried,
because we're near the
end of the chapter,
and when we're on the
outside again,
We'll drink a Guinness
with rapture,
we'll put on the headphones,
and listen to some tunes,
Metallica, AC/DC,
We'll be over the moon,
So, fuck you all,
we're not a rat to be tested,
we'll find a lovely lesbian,
and really molest it!

'03

Space

Trapped on a mat determined
to be kept flat,
one night's admission
turns into a week,
drugs are numbing that
I can hardly speak,
I'm becoming a drone with a
confused, depressed tone,
people keep talking, it's
hard to stay in a zone.
Is it the acid, or is it the meds?
The acid I took when I was in bed,
On the outside, I was being
filled with dreads,
I hear a voice in Dublin
after visiting a church,
saying with the vision
of a woman's head,
"We will fill him dread."

'03

Storm in a tea cup

When the fluid in the cup leaves,
the tea is gone,
but there is a mystery
left that weaves,
into the future,
and out of the past,
but only a discerning eye,
will know how to cast,
what was lost,
but not forgotten,
what was gained,
but left for rotten,

so, appreciate with gratitude,
your hidden talent and vocation,
because it's all real life,
shot on location.

02/08/03

Liverpool F.C

Forget your Man Utd,
And especially Everton,
People only support them,
as a pastime or for a little fun!
Cos there's only one team,
that beats them all for spirit,
and outdoes them all,
and I'm not talking
about the Arsenal!
They may be the Gunners,
but they're the second
place runners,
like Everton,
- they missed their
morning Coffees,
And then they wonder why,
they're called the toffees?!!
Cos unlike Liverpool,
they're very unstable,
and always stuck,
to the bottom of the table!!!
The 'pool is the best,
they're a class act,
and that's a sincere statement,
I'd never retract,
Forget your Rooney,
Cos we've got Owen,
and low and behold,
he's not yet fully grown,
So, apostasy to the rest,
sit and spin,
Cos we are the BEST
and we're out to WIN!!!

02/08/03

Favourite things

A favourite thing can
be of many sorts,
If it's not to your liking,
Well, then you can abort.
If it's a song you like,
that you play over and over,
or your wee pet dog,
whose name is Rover,
a minor pleasure in life,
not to all or everyone's liking,
but it raises a passion in you,
as in an angry Viking.
The passion and feeling,
this thing does cause,
makes you stop in your tracks,
It makes life pause.
Not just a pastime,
to while away the hours,
It could be stamp collecting,
or picking of flowers,
but it's unique to you,
and when it's unavailable,
it turns you blue,
It's a favourite thing,
or it could be plural,
Like the silence of a winter's night,
somewhere rural,
It creates inner peace,
And gives you breathing space,
a break from reality,
and the whole human RACE!

03/08/03

Concert

It's concert day,
hip-hip hooray,
Will I get out?
You're fucking right I will,
Whatever it takes,
If it means blood to spill,
but I'd prefer a peaceful exit,
although I have to return,
because the passion inside,
is on the eternal burn.
So, I need a release,
don't fence me in,
to do it to me,
would be a terrible SIN!,
I gotta feel the beat,
the sweating of bodies,
and feel the heat!,
Stand in the queue,
Waiting for my non-
alcoholic drink,
those youngsters drinking,
will get sick I think!!
But listen to the song,
and hear the words,
I've to go to the toilet,
Ughh!! Look at those turds!!!
Is there no cleaner?
Because there is defo a screener,
he took my stash,
coming in the gate,
but the music's a substitute,
it'll HAVE TO compensate!!!

04/08/03

Fran

Life and strife,
trouble in a bubble,
but it's your little sphere,
so stop trying to hang yourself,
and for most people,
it's something they hold dear.
It's fragile and valuable,
and quite easy to bust,
so, if you feel it's over,
can't take anymore,
Well out with the rope,
and then you must,
Personally, I feel
it's the cowardly option,
think of your parents,
of your brother and sister,
and dead in heaven,
and how much you missed her,
If not for yourself,
why put them through it?
It's the ultimate in selfishness,
when you DIY or BBQ it,
because the aspect of things,
that are most important to us,
are often clouded and shrouded,
in a veil of dust.
Ashes to ashes,
or jumping off bridges,
intentional car crashes,
Chicken shit fuckers,
get over your strife,
just find your position,
in this wonderful LIFE!

05/08/03

Escape!

Escape to freedom,
Escape & flee,
Escape to the outside,
For victory!
The first hurdle is simple,
like squeezing a blackhead pimple,
But when on the run,
Evade the gun,
evade the capture,
for glorious rapture,
Left behind is the fence,
as I make haste with my pence,
left behind in my cabin,
is all of my scents,
As I run, I've got with me,
all that I need,
as I put the head down,
and crank up the speed,
They'll never catch me,
I'm too bloody smart,
fuck them anyway,
I wouldn't give them the
smell of my fart,
The second hurdle now,
without drawing attention,
is to get some money,
an overdraft extension!!!
More bang for your buck,
like I give a fuck,
I'm now kitted out,
in a righteous rig,
a coupla of beers, and
I'm off the gig!!!

05/08/03

Bending the rules

Well fuck me pink,
We're not fucking kids,
what the hell do you think?
I'll have to grab your heads,
and stick them in the sink.
I'll turn on with the hot,
then on with the cold,
What's that, you say?
"Get to bed – do as your told?",
Snowballs chance in hell,
is what I will tell you,
I've never done it before,
Well, not that I'm aware of,
but my parents are masters,
in the art of bluff,
So unbeknownst to me,
it might have occurred,
but for you 'all to tell me,
is pretty absurd,
It stretches my patience,
beyond new realms like a catapult,
We're not fucking children,
I'm a fully grown adult!!!!
So, don't patronize or chastise,
or look at me with those eyes,
or talk with a sympathetic voice,
If you bend a few rules,
then we can all
REJOICE!!

17/08/03

This is what I was on in St. Pat's mental asylum. Fucking shit, hey? This where I had the allergic reaction to Serenace and nearly bloody died.

3 x Serenace 10mg
Lithium 20mg(400ml)

Relax

Relax and feel good,
take your drugs,
it'll lighten your mood,
Oops, a daisy,
we gave you the wrong ones,
golly gosh,
it made you crazy,
sorry about that,
my mistake,
it's funny how it made your body,
rattle like a snake.
Brain is spinning,
it won't stay still,
it's okay, though,
we have for you a downer pill,
we'll strike a balance,
through trial and terror,
again don't worry,
but you won't know your
own reflection,
in your own mirror,
but it's good for you,
cos we know best ;),
you might not know it,
but we are in the business
of reading minds,
and we don't like your happiness,
you're too full of zest,
well I say, fuck you,
fuck them,
and burn the Rest!

17/08/03

Believe

Do you believe it?
Cos I believe it's true,
but what's the question,
Am I telling you?
It's a rhetoric retort
of an age old conundrum,
an answer of a sort.
To believe in yourself,
I believe in myself,
watch this space,
see me blast into orbit,
and at last, I'll be free,
the true colours will shine,
and they'll all be yours & mine,
I'll use it for good,
to help my friends and family,
they may not know where
they stand now,
but they know where they stood,
I take them at face value,
cos I love and trust them all,
they stand up for what they believe,
they stand proud and tall.
They'll begin to believe,
when they see the real me,
my capabilities and acumen,
will astound and amaze,
hidden talents I secreted away,
away from the world's view,
so, give them 3D glasses,
and let them GAZE!!!

17/08/03

Sit and spin!
Ages 6 to 9

AA

The aunt @ the back,
said anxiety attack,
poor uncle Neil,
I know how you feel,
Cos we've got one, two,
peas in a pod,
twins from hell,
or sometimes God,
bad enough on their own,
but with their forces combined,
it's impossible to unwind,
you gotta close your ears,
as they talk at each other,
it is a scene that would raise a smile,
on a man who is blind.
In vino veritas,
as they spill their news,
and the rest of us look on,
and sing the blues.
My favourite model auntie,
dressed to the nines with style,
at Christmas and birthdays,
she arrives with presents by the pile,
for an uncle and aunt
you couldn't meet better,
they're straight to the point,
just like a red setter,
so, 'til I see them,
they'll Carpe Diem!

19/08/03

CONcise

My mental state,
I try to encapsulate,
within my poem & song,
Can't you read between the lines?
Can't anyone see what's going on?
I explain it as concisely
as anyone could,
but it falls on deaf ears,
are people's heads like wood?
Would they let me go if,
like normal, I act?
Or give me a little,
then retract?
It's fucking me up,
inside within,
I try to find the words,
but don't know where to begin,
I'll try again,
I like one, and one is two,
I'll take out my calculator,
even better – an abacus,
but tractatus – logico Philosophicus,
it's selective listening,
they can't see what I feel,
cos only what I let them,
is what they think for real,
well, in the weeks I will be gone,
but you'll be stuck here for
your whole life LONG!

20/08/03

Gone?

So is Flo gone?
Am I like W.B Yeats?
Whose Maud is Gonne?
I think she's gone for a while,
but not forever,
something did click,
that would take a lot to sever,
likeness of a mind,
thoughts and feelings,
that was spoken to digress,
freedom of speech,
and speak to be free,
a kindred bird without wings,
yet and maybe only,
into flings,
it came at a time,
which we truly needed,
and WHEN we had the feeling,
with which to feed it,
it may have been love,
for a very short time,
but she hasn't let go,
as I rightly know,
the action and not the words,
the depth in a short time,
how it all came about,
how it all occurred,
if I'll move on and so might she,
we'll meet on the other side,
as Grampa did say,
c'est la vie!

'03

I Con

All in a lifetime, as Daddy does say,
Do I go with the flow,
and in God, we pray?
Or grab the bull by the horns,
and decide my own fate!
The first one sounds easy,
the last one sounds real,
stand up and be counted,
show them your steel!
It's an individualistic attitude,
to set you apart,
to find your own path
and make your mark,
self-fulfillment through selfless acts,
to be held in the same light,
and respected as he,
too much to ask for?
I have to wait and see,
Misguided opinions on
other people's thoughts,
how others see you as
you see yourself,
What I've craved for as a boy,
and now as man,
is the respect from others,
that I think I've earned,
but not as a madman or
wildcard in the pack,
but as a serious contender
who's on the right track!

23/08/03

Anything

If I write about anything,
it'll still be about something,
No matter where I stop,
No matter what the stage,
Unless I don't write anything
and give you a blank page,
So, if you have a subject,
Something or anything
to write upon,
and I don't mean paper,
cos that would be wrong,
I have my own paper,
So, once I have it,
I'll write you a poem,
or even a song,
I hope it's not too late.
Have you already gone?
Is that a coincidence
or just fate?
I believe in fate and
also in luck,
Cos there's too many coincidences,
that would fill a truck!!!
So, have a safe journey,
all through your life,
Cos I sense in you,
You'll beat this strife,
So let me hear you sing,
I CAN do ANYTHING!!!

24/08/03

Imprisonment

Every minute is like an eternity.
Have you ever been locked up?
It can be quite scary!
Freedom is one of the many
things I hold dear,
although normally joking...
about this, I'm quite sincere.
If you don't have your freedom,
what have you got?
A city full of cars,
but an empty parking lot!
They can get in,
but we can't get out,
you can walk to the gate,
but then right turn about!
Back in your box,
jack the lad,
I don't care if you're just happy,
this'll make you sad!
Well, you know what?
No matter how they try,
they won't change me,
I don't care how you swot,
pearls of wisdom,
rolling down your face,
I don't care if we've only met,
up where I come from,
we call it sweat,
so, sweat all you want,
gimme those pills,
I'll sit and I'll smile,
at the world sitting on
the window sills,
it's not them I'm after,
it's just life's thrills!!!

25/08/03

Love & Depression

Love & depression,
a psychotic session,
Is it real love
or just an obsession?
Well, not long ago,
you really found out,
you had another argument,
and she hit you a clout!
Was it a thump down?
On top of the head?
That was your heartbreaking,
You internally bled!
Love is one thing,
depression is another,
so take one at a time,
or you'll be pretty confused,
like a twin & his brother,
So take it easy,
give life a chance,
moderation in drink,
and you'll happily dance,
The double A meeting,
is not a passing thought,
it's hardly fleeting,
skip out the drugs,
it's only for mugs,
Depress your heart,
let it inflate,
try using laughter,
to COMPENSATE!

26/08/03

Eternal Itch

Itchy and scratchy,
can leave you all patchy,
the eternal itch,
from the open wound.
Swollen full of anger,
like an inflated balloon,
it's red and irritating,
Will it ever fucking heal?
If they keep me locked up,
then under lock and key,
is how I'm gonna feel.
Is my nails sharp enough,
or do they need a buff,
Or do you think I look very tough?
On the outside, I look as
hard as nails or the like,
but deep on the inside,
I'm just one big sharpened spike!
So please don't anger me,
or I'll turn you into a skewer,
cos there's none more pure,
than a repentant whore.
But fuck y'all,
I'm gonna have some fun,
So I'll light my ass,
And blow y'all to Kingdom come!!!

27/08/03

Lots of love Kena

Juan by nature, and Juan by name,
He's as true as they come
but not all that sane,
With his funky wee hat,
that sits on his head,
As he bops along to his 'Eminem',
He's fit as they come,
I'm telling you now,
Defo for a fling,
And as for that bum,
So Juan by name but and by nature,
You better watch that bum,
Coz I'm coming to take her!!!

27/08/03

Snatchet

Bereft of personality,
when personality is key,
subtract the drugs,
and you'll still find me.
You've gotta make an allowance,
for my happy go lucky ambience,
but I won't put up with
this shit forever,
so someone will soon shout
for an ambulance.
I'll say one thing for
free...Fuck you!!
It won't be for me!
So, show me you've studied,
how to avoid your nose
being bloodied,
Or are you a sheep or a robot?
Put together with a
socket and ratchet,
Cos if you don't show me soon,
I'll dismantle you and your dreams,
with a big fucking hatchet!!
So, fuck you motherfuckers,
When I see my chance for freedom,
I'm gonna snatchet!!!

27/08/03

Fuck the models Kena

I've only just met you,
and I think you're really sound,
I love your eyes,
they're really bright and round,
I can see inside them,
a true sign of intelligence,
but this fear of being fat,
you'll have to dispense.
If you lose any more weight,
it'll destroy that lovely
figure then hence,
because contrary to woman's belief,
men prefer their ladies bigger!
What I can't figure out,
is who told you all
skinny was good?
It's the truth Kena,
I blame the fucking of supermodels,
for promoting lack of growth,
All everyone needs is exercise,
because what you see & read,
is all a load of codswallop,
Exercise to stay in shape,
to keep you fit and keep you light,
so, take care of yourself,
and nice to that body of yours,

and if people piss you off
for being good looking,
Well fuck them,
They belong in the
SEWERS!!

28/08/03

What attracted you me 2 u?

Me 2 you,
And you 2 me,
The attraction is obvious,
a blind man could see,
We're not looking for love,
from heaven above,
just a quick shag,
a release from the bag,
and it's between you and me,
so, we're not allowed to brag!
A bit of excitement,
a change from the norm,
Some TLC,
Sex like lightening,
from a thunderstorm,
Loving that's quick,
yet also slow,
touching and feelings,
that excite the soul,
So, I tell you now,
what attracted me 2 you,
without a doubt,
It was defo your mind,
I wanted to fuck your brains OUT!

29/08/03

Back to reality?

So what's next
After this game?
Is it back to normal
or more of the same?
No drugs or eavesdropping,
or peering eyes,
I can be myself,
no need for a lock and key.
I can show my brilliance,
leave it all in the past,
as a distant memory,
Forget myself a little,
if only a little at a time,
there are boundries,
like a pitch with lime.
Stay within the realm of society,
but bollocks to that!
It just ain't me,
I'll be myself,
without the added hi
but I'm still gonna soar,
I'll still rise and fly,
Phoenix from your flames,
inside the reality,
Don't try and rationalize,
or put me in a box,
I'm the odd one out,
in 10 billion pairs of socks!!!

30/08/03

Evolution

And so, it starts,
a new beginning,
a clean sheet, fresh page,
a chance for winning,
a different song,
a brand-new tune,
a future bright,
a forthcoming attraction,
in the cinemas soon,
a star of the future,
a blinding shine,
a discarder of be-grudgers,
let them FUCKING whine.
A drinker of beer,
a tippler of delights,
Can you see my name?
It's up in lights,
I prefer it down to earth,
written in drunken piss,
cos I'm a down to earth guy,
you don't want to miss,
a playboy to millions,
a lover to a few,
I should only have one,
but sure 15 sure what can ye do?!
No money in the bank,
but piles in my arse,
I don't need a penny,
they're just a farce.
I'll drive my Ferrari,
and tell my mother, not to worry!!!!

30/07/03

Golf

You first strike the pose,
as everyone knows,
Then check your stance,
and address the ball,
hit it with rhythm,
and watch it rise and fall,
Where it lands,
depends on your direction,
and for men, if it lands right,
there's a possible erection,
but woman are cooler,
Cos they play consistently,
without any huff,
a good shot, bad shot,
or if it lands on the rough,
They play the percentage,
not like the men,
Who blast it for the pin,
and end up in it again.
But as the men get older,
they start losing their balls,
and playing like their old wives,
makes them bang their heads
off the walls!
It's a great game to play,
I love the scent of the grass,
I love playing with my friends,
and kicking their ass!!
Drive for show & putt
for dough,
On the 18th -,
it's the conclusive club,
a nice little gimme,
And it's into the PUB!!!

ST. PAT'S MENTAL ASYLUM 2 – THE SEROQUEL

15/01/04

Reason?

What's it all about?
This life of ours?
It twists in turns,
and sometimes sours,
Sometimes slow,
then the speed of light,
no matter your problem,
no matter your plight,

takes the feet from under you,
then gives you the wings to fly,
moves you to tears,
then laugh till you cry,

So, what's it all about?
The answer's there is none,
to make you scream and shout,
But surely there's a reason,
for what's done and intended?
Continue your plans,
until they're up-ended?
Or don't plan at all,
and come what may,
ignore all advice and direction,
no matter what they say?

That would not do,
cause then you'd drift,
and in no time at all,
you'd be on the heavenly lift,

So, give yourself your own reason,
for this life you lead,
and if you get good advice,
then surely take heed,

But if you still seek the reason,
a simple one will suffice,
don't worry, it's just fate,
and not the role of the dice.

11/07/04

Eileen

A crazy young man named Juan,
Refused to keep his clothes on,
So, he pulled off his drawers,
they sent for the lawyers,
But he legged it with
no trousers on!

08/08/04

Irish summers

D'ye ever wake up in the morning,
and look at the sky?
And think to yourself,
what a lovely Irish day?
Then half way down the road,
you think, why oh why?
Where once was sunshine,
rain hits you on the nose,
but it's not the weather's fault,
you just wore the wrong clothes.
As Billy Connolly stated,
there's no such thing
as bad weather,
if you think that it gets you down,
and turns a happy face into a frown,
You're in Ireland, for God sake,
don't complain, pull
yourself together,
After all, it's only weather.

08/08/04

This was written while incarcerated for the first time in St Pat's mental asylum in Dublin against my will. They would not listen and still don't. I tell the truth - that I faked Bipolar. I was told to go to bed by Sarah like a good little boy cos it was past my bedtime.

And that she doesn't make the law, she just enforces it (I was 25!). She means well, but there's room for common sense in every walk of life! (all written on the original)

0352hrs.....Bedtime

Archimedes said...."Give me
a fulcrum large enough, a
lever long enough,
and a place to stand....and I
will move the world."
When I read these words,
in my mind its provoked thoughts,
sent shivers down my spine,
and sent a chill to my
toes that curled.
So, all I ask is a pen that's
mightier than the sword,
And I will write the speech
of the written word.
It may invoke thought,
and send a rumble
through your brain,
but it's not impossible to think
so hard that you'll go insane!
So listen to every word
of what people say,
It may improve your life and
help you out someday.

08/08/04

This was written later on that morning after writing "0352hrs...Bedtime".

Words of scrabble

Sitting right here now in
the morning still,
listening to the birds and
their first light shrill,
the drone of the traffic
drundling by,
the reason behind the question,
Becomes less and less why?
But more of an answer
the more I learn,
and the worries of people
become less of a concern.
They're starting to believe as
long as I don't go too fast,
and someday very soon,
the knowledge we impart
will stay fixed and last.

09/08/04

Sleep

Summertime is a field of dreams,
tied up after harvesting,
in a mind without seams,
You wake in the morning,
with all the joys of life,
maybe look to the future,
for a husband or wife,
if already married,
then a future together,
but all of these thoughts,
come from the
summertime weather.

09/08/04

I was inspired to go to Trinity college to do computer's by Xanadu whom you possibly read blew more than my mind in iCon.

Trinity college?

So you want to go there?
Why ever for?
Well, my friend from
the sea is there,
studying Maths and French,
and he said I might find,
myself a good wench.
She'll be smart, she'll be funny,
whatever about her looks,
but talent for thought provoke,
you won't rebuke,
it's a great atmosphere,
to immerse yourself in,
and if you want the best out of life,
then this is where to begin.
No matter what you study,
from keyhole surgery to knitting,
they'll fill your brain,
till the sides are splitting,
so I took on-board what he said,
and thought to myself,
while lying in bed,
that's me,
sign me up,
where do I pay?
Carpe diem,
Grasp the day!

20/08/04

Who, me, I...?

So, you think you know me?
or so you say,
to underestimate me,
would be a regrettable day,
Not for me,
But most definitely you,
A condescending attitude,
that would make some people sue,
So, you know my mind?
Even sussed out my thinking,
realized with ease,
why I was always drinking,
Taking some herb,
Medicinal dope,
yet I confuse the hell out of ye,
when I say, God bless the Pope!
You see your problem is,
now I'm not telling you your job,
ye've got ears but don't listen,
that's your prob,
If we use 10% of our brain,
that leaves 90 uncharted,
yet you say you know me,
Don't get me started,
if you don't know yourself,
how can you know me?
I see doubt in your eyes,
It's like you're lost @ sea,
up shit creak in a barbed
wire canoe,
oh no, we've sprung a leak,
what can we do?
Bucket less, paddleless,
look at the hole,
The secrets to my life,
are under lock and key in my soul.

20/08/04

bUNI-polar

Bipolar or Uni,
or out and out loony,
so, I dropped my trousers,
and showed her a moony,
the trousers were mental,
a metaphor, so to speak,
and when I said what I said,
threw her fingers she did peak,
her question arose from the
book of words mind,
the answer was in there,
but with blinkers on,
people do go blind,
she said, you're not Uni-polar,
there's no such thing,
Ah! Ha! said my head,
ding a ling ling,
so, I asked her a question,
"there's no Uni, but there's Bi?"
Yes, she said, and I'll tell you why,
but I interrupted,
and told her I only go high,
but she interrupted back,
and said "let me explain"
with a frown,
said she you're telling me,
you don't go down?
I said I'd stay down all day,
to which she was affronted,
probably a little turned on,
but embarrassment took over,
cause I'd certainly hit
the right buttons,
that definitely drove her,
then insult to injury,
I couldn't let it lie,
cause if you do that,
opportunities pass you by,
so, I told her to warn the doc,
it doesn't exist,
and in all his years of reading,
there's something he missed,
this startled her a bit,
or should I say a bit more,
a double whammy in 3 minutes,
is quite a good score,
but I told her not to worry,
and that I would set him straight,
but she insisted they'd confer,
so, they both can enjoy the bait!

'04

Bunnies

I've let you undress me,
within your mind's eye,
I didn't let you,
It's yours for the taking,
and fantasy making,
but not hearts breaking,
friends forever,
fuck buddies of a kind,
but I need no other,
cause I have you in my mind.

10/08/04

Cut grass

Is he killing the grass,
or helping it grow?
With every stroke of the blade,
in slow mow,
the scent comes forth,
and fills the air,
and is as pleasing to the nostrils,
as a woman's fresh washed hair,

but the grass is like the Irish,
it's green to the core,
and unlike the grass,
we will be bullied no MORE!

14/08/04

Love won

What's love?
Is it sent from heaven?
Or lying dormant in the heart?
Awaiting activation,
amalgamation with your other part?
When this is done,
it's then it does start,
Every second,
of every minute,
the whole day through,
It gets harder all the time,
without seeing you,
Yet when we're together,
it's eternal bliss,
Our love and sense
soar exponentially,
the independent body,
might abscond,
but the heart follows mentally,
The trees and the grass,
and the lovely flowers,
are part & parcel,
Of Gods powers,
This gives me love,
Whether it's hail, rain, or shine,
like drilling a hole in Ethiopia,
to get water from the mine,
I truly believe,
it turns the world in a spin,
But you must work in harmony,
and give love a chance to
WIN!

14/08/04

Love

Some recognize lust for true love,
Sent from heaven by a dove,
but I know now where to begin,
cos she slaps me on the
ass and says you're in,
and whispers in my ear,
"you're in love!"

15/08/04

Cuckoo

It's not very often,
you hear the cuckoo,
when you hear voices in your head,
what do you do?
You reach for a spliff,
and take a good whiff,
and your life doesn't look like poo.

15/08/04

Much ado about nothing

Before I came in,
there was no sign of rot,
Just relax and unwind,
but now I've almost forgot,
my intentions were paramount,
for my artistic flow,
oh God, I wish I had,
some hash for a chill pill blow,
It should be prescribed,
for those who won't react,
I'm sincere in these words,
So, my statement I won't retract,
for fuck sakes a diversion,

of any kind,
Can't you see we're idle,
Are you motherfucking blind,
So, get your act together,
have a tool box talk,
Stop being as predictable
as the weather!
and thick as a block.

15/08/04

Sandals

I'm gonna hitch around
Ireland in sandals,
no doubt that'll cause
some scandals,
But they were made for walking,
to facilitate talking,
And I grip them with
my feet like handles.

17/08/04

The Closet has been deskeletised

A problem shared is a
problem halved,
So, the more people I tell,
the greater the division will be,
so much so,
it'll be an ever decreasing
circle of 10 -n,
The big bang occurred last year,
but now I'm in the refining stages,
there's a bit to go,
but I'm getting there,
With the burden gone,
life moves on,
it tried to drag me down,
and look like a clown,
but I stood up to be counted,
and my white horse I mounted,
I've done the crime,
and I've done my time,
And they're possibly right,
that it doesn't pay,
but fuck it!
Who cares?
Hi ho silver away!!!

18/08/04

I called this group therapy as a joke amongst the other patients. We were all sitting in the sitting room. About 7 of us. We bounced off each other and called out one line each as I wrote them down.

Party hats

Another year has gone,
We stick them on our heads,
always so small and cute,
Sometimes as night
caps in our beds,
let's all sing a happy party song,
No-one knows the words,
before we know, they'll all be gone,
What will the year bring?
Buddha bangs his gong.
With the partyers in their throng,
Some of them stripey,
in a mood where nothing
seems wrong,
They don't stop to question why?
As in ecstasy, they fly,
Higher than their minds
can ever perceive,

Are you Niamh?
Open your minds and
hands to receive,
open your hearts, and
you'll never grieve,
Pretell why fret,
surrounded by beauty,
how can we forget,
It's not a big stone where
everything is set,
It's more of a river to
which eternity flows,
It's got its own trade winds
that perpetually blows.

18/08/04

Perfect

The pen hits the page,
and followed its course,
without any rage,
free flowing like a river,
from the mountain top,
it tracks its own path,
without any stop,
weaving and eroding,
to river, estuary and the sea,
it has no boundries,
I wish it were me,
The world as your oyster,
3/4's of the planet,
what a lovely place it would be,
if the right person run it,
Judgement through experience,
experience through time,
perfection unattainable,
Yet rid the world of slime,
Eutopia's a dream,
but we don't live in a pipe,
we pluck the apples,
when they're ready and ripe,
Some say wait till they fall,
Cos they're waiting for perfection,
but I say, "Catch it
while it's flying!",
It's just natural selection.

18/08/04

Picture perfect

Can something really
be picture perfect?
Because every time you look at it,
It invokes a different effect,
So, maybe it's not the picture,
it's more about the mood,
the angle and perspective,
of each and every time you stood,
the landscapes of the mountains,
two men on the move standing still,
they're stopped mid-stride,
are they dragging their
turf or making a still?
Well, we are all in lovely Ireland,
So, let's stack all the bloody turf,
then go and drink our bloody fill.

19/08/04

14 lines

As I sat on it,
I thought of a sonnet,
but the job is not over,
till the paper works done,
When I flush away the waste,
my pen and paper will be at one,
to scroll the scribe,

from the calligraphy tribe,
I'll write the words,
from the inscriptions that hide,
I hope it's free to access,
because I've no money for a bribe!
Ah! Now I remember the
nubile young girl at the gate,
maybe she'll let me in if I
take her out for a date.

19/08/04

Horses

What an event!
Is she for sale or rent?
She doesn't trot, she glides,
look at the sheen of her body,
a perfect hide among hides.
She's fizzing up now,
She knows what's ahead,
keep her cool for the dressage,
Or our chances are dead,
The dressage is over,
So, let's let her at it,
The jumping gene's there,
She's clear without a hit,
A sight to behold,
A sight for sore eyes,
With a horse like this,
We can reach for the Skies!

19/08/04

Trinity

Qualified people,
to show you inside and out,
and to check out your teammates,
and see who's about,
The Durac injection,
is a yearly unravel,
for sports equipment,
some coaching,
affiliation and travel,
On or Off campus doesn't matter,
Cause we always teach
you from scratch,
just unlocking that good
brain of yours,
Then merely lifting the latch,
And with a face lift on
Luce sports centre,
it's looking rather smart,
indoor sports,
And martial arts,
as every style in existence,
is very close to my heart,
With cardiovascular resistance,
for and against the machines,
We must learn to control them,
before they develop some jeans,
2 mile upstream,
painted better than knew,
is the ladies and men's boat club,
@ Santry avenue,
But for me, 5 miles north,
is where my hidden
talent will unfurl,
the minute I see those goal posts,
and the second I touch that sacred
HURL!!!

19/08/04

Cricket - Trinity

Serious or not,
inter-club or recreational,
we've got the lot,

a stranger's a friend,
you just haven't met,
there are meetings and groups,
4 dimensions don't forget.
And after these gatherings,
there's always a time extension,
for intermingling, flesh pressing,
ice breaking the tension,
at the crest of the wave,
progress to another,
new life, new sport,
there's 45 to choose from,
one or the other,
so, it's down to you,
cause only you can pick it,
I'd recommend all of them,
especially the cricket,
yeah, it's in the category of sports,
it just gets bad press,
because of the English,
who tried to oppress,
but without auld Vicky,
the college wouldn't exist,
so, for inspirational people,
she's top of the list.

20/08/04

Player/Manager

They say fame and fortune,
is all about timing,
and poems and songs,
are all about rhyming,
what if all this thinking
was turned on its head,
Would you be up for a revolution,
if I told you a secret that
some might dread?
It's not a bad thing,
it's really pretty good,
now I'm not kissing your ass,
from the off that must
be understood.
I see these young girl/boy bands,
singing about shit, they
know nothing about,
and it's not their fault,
It's just whoever has the clout,
so I decided to myself,
unbeknownst to anyone,
that I'd hide myself till thirty,
then I'd knock on the
door and in I'd come,
As you know yourself,
the reason you left the band,
it was becoming less inspiring,
going through the motions,
and kind of somewhat bland,
So I gave myself to thirty,
to make history of my own,
and a lifetime of material,
that would surely keep me going,
but now I'm 26 and I feel
I've reached that place,
to write, sing songs and dance,
with my audience of
the human race,
I'm sure you're wondering by now,
why the hell I'm writing to you?
the reasons pretty simple,
it's because you're starting anew,
you'll be open to new ideas,
not just that,
but you'll teach me some,
unlike some in your business,
inflicted with verbal diarrhoea,
full of shit up to their armpit,
that's not what I want,
I'll keep my feet on the ground,

which I believe you and your
good wife have done,
so, if I do my stuff,
will you make me No. 1???

'08/04

Pole

If you say Uni,
doesn't that mean everyone?
I forget who I told,
somebody said somebody,
anyone, someone,
so why when about the polar,
3 halves it's shared as one?
You've up polar,
down polar,
Bipolar being 2,
and,
Unipolar being one,
So how can Uni be everyone?
Anyone, who one, do one,
Then just jump right back,
saying fuck this!
It's not what I wanted,
only as one when we were one,
the last time it happened,
Was it flaunted?
We conquered the pole,
So, to Columbus and
to backpackers,
We're now all a United whole!
Pole united could be
our Gaelic team,
on my journey here,
I thought of Tom Creen.

20/08/04

The Scooby doo ending

..........the way's just
around the corner,
the road to redemption's
a rocky one,
to say the least,
but nibble on all advice,
then hoard it all together for a feast.
The light at the end of the tunnel,
is not an on-coming train,
So, if you need to
cleanse your body,
walk naked in the rain,
Sip from the fountain
of knowledge,
put closure on that pain,
Clear your conscience for freedom,
don't let it drive you insane,
Think happy thoughts,
No matter how hard that may be,
But your future will look bright,
So, suck it and see!!!

22/08/04

Written for Doyler who didn't pay for his parking ticket when he came to visit me.

Free admission

The parking permit,
is in the post,
but I've always got some space,
and I'm a gracious host,
Phantom of the opera,
or forever a ghost?
It's now up to you,
to make the most.

23/08/04

Radiation

When you look in the mirror,
What do you see?
Is it a true reflection,
that's felt within thee?
All these problems and issues,
bottled up inside,
bursting at the seams,
yet trying to hide,
So, here's a thought,
Why not do what the
mirror just did?
Slide your baggage along
the reflection,
to where the emanations are hid,
Cleanse your body,
free your mind and soul,
Get closure on that bad boy,
put him back in his box,
and nail the lid.

23/08/04

Scratch

The taxi awaits,
@ the Golden gates,
inviting, enticing,
Weaving and splicing,
thoughts in my mind,
of the escape kind,
but I know there's no point,
because when you're
eventually caught,
you're back in the joint,
The decks are cleared,
and you start from scratch,
it's all a game,
it's just a match,
keep your head down,
and an eye on the scoreboard,
You've plenty of time to recover,
that you can afford.

23/08/04

Unito

Into the outside,
outside to the in,
it's inside out,
when the outsides in.
Where to begin?
Oh, where to get in??
Begin at the start,
when starting a beginning,
first impressions last,
so you need a formula 4 winning,
talk in their subject,
talk in their tongue,
explain to everyone,
that their foot is on the rung,
And that there is one definite thing,
that is defo in life,
no matter how your hat is hung,
no matter what they say or tell,
you're the air that feeds the lung.

24/08/04

Fianna Never Fail

All I can say,
Is up Donegal!
We tried and failed,
but we did not fall,
McEniffs men,

all done us proud,
So, if you're from Donegal,
Stand tall and shout it loud,
Our Tir Chonnaill Gladiators,
learned some rugby moves,
it didn't work this year,
but they're only finding
their groves,
So, watch this space,
we will rise to the top,
A skill and aggression onslaught,
that'll be impossible to stop.

24/08/04

Stereo

Lyrics flax the air,
Exacting opinions,
from the crowd that's there,
I go pretty blank,
when I try to think of something,
but the words of songs,
make me sing,
and when I speak,
there's not a sound,
you could hear a penny ping,
The words that travel in my voice,
the opinions of millions,
And they've all come before me,
to dance and rejoice,
They sing and dance table-tapping,
that stereo tattoo,
that was until this very day,
a by-lawed, outlawed,
didgery-doo taboo.

24/08/04

The Office!

Ground control to teacher Tom,
It wasn't me, t'was the computer,
there appears to be something
in there gone wrong,
I hit this, and I hit this,
so many times,
I have the bleeps in my head,
like nursery rhymes,
Well says Tom,
it's very much the same,
if you treat it all like
playing a game,
don't approach the unit,
with utmost sheer terror,
fear no queries,
because sometimes it's not,
an operator error,
so, take your time and forget,
the lord's name in vein,
practice makes perfect,
and the better you'll be,
the more you train.

25/08/04

The happy family law solicitor who's Bipolar and recovering from alchoholism

Solicit your body,
Solicit your mind,
Solicit your happiness,
So, listen and find,
speak after thinking,
or your family will go blind,

Like the boy who cried wolf,
Bipolar or not,
if you're in the constant limelight,
you will not forget,
champagne income,
doesn't mean the same lifestyle,
because it'll all unravel,
after a while,
so, head above water,
will help you recover,
and don't rule out all men,
you need at least one lover,
to start your own family,
and make some laws of your own,
and when you've done that,
you have fully grown.

25/08/04

Cigarette butts

The very last drag,
at the end of the fag,
it's the end of one,
and the start of another,
Can I burn a fag for ye?
Said my fellow brother,
I'll leave you my butt,
said the guy's mother,
Cigarettes are bad for ye,
I've told ye before,
We've all known that,
Since the days of yore!
Do as I say,
not as I do,
you'll live a longer life,
when the cigarette butts are few.

26/08/04

Embalmed

They've finally arrived,
on their jet plane,
after years and years,
of again and again,
The promises cousin's make,
of meeting each other,
but now they're here,
sister to sister & one another,
you're looking well, says the
Irish man to the yank,
have you been embalmed?
Is the secret of life
enclosed in your hand?
Do you use the power
to wash your body all over,
it looks timeless and ageless,
there's a sheen from your coat,
that's just like rover!

26/08/04

It is as it is

The red hand of Ulster says No!
But the green hand of
Ireland says yes,
but before we argue,
let us digress,
It was ours before,
And it still is ours now,
so, when you think about it,
Why the big row?
You stole it from us,
under a false pretence,
We had depression from oppression,
and limited defence,

It's a different story now,
from those by-gone days,
We're all shining bright,
just look @ our rays,
Every corner of the earth,
has a little Irish in them,
Your empire is no more,
there's very few left for
you to condemn,
Our point is made,
so, give it back,
if not my vengeance,
you will exact,
There's many more like me,
Who'll support the 6
counties expense,
I hope it doesn't go too far,
but attack is the best
form of defence.

These are a selection of quotes enjoyed by Janie – my romantic interlude partner

- Education is an admirable thing, but it is well to remember from time to time that nothing that is worth knowing can be taught.

- He hadn't a single redeeming vice.

- Most people are other people. Their thoughts are someone else's opinions, their lives a mimicry, their passions a quotation.
  - Oscar Wilde

- This is one race of people for whom psychoanalysis is of no use what-so-ever.
  - Freud on the Irish

Only Irish coffee provides in a single glass all four essential food groups: alcohol, caffeine, sugar, and fat
  - Alex Levine

27/08/04

Borderline

All the boundaries,
and lines,
within the confines of,
your apparent liberty,
disinhibited free mind.
Who says they knew?
Are they sure it was you?
Ah, it's yourself, how do ye do?
But back to the question,
cos we side stepped & flew,
and if you do it again,
I'll turn the airwaves blue,
and flutter around this compound,
like a coked-up cuckoo,
So, you knew all along?
But didn't say?
no-one ever asked,
they just let me play,
I was encouraged at home,
but restricted at school,
I didn't like rules,
and enjoyed playing the fool,
so, to those who called me a waster,
let this be a little taster,
the tip of the iceberg,
on your tongue,
and I'll write and sing the verse,
of the songs that are yet unsung.

Bread head

Fresh from the head,
like freshly cooked bread,
don't shine too brightly,
or expect something frightfully,
it's happened to me,
all of my life,
my device was to rhyme,
and I do mean strife,
hospital once,
but now it's been twice,
now you've bipolar illness,
and it's not like lice,
you can't have a good wash,
and it'll all be gone,
you must cleanse your soul,
at the stroke of dawn,
a new day to progress and strive,
every time you wake up
and take a breath,
it's a good day to be alive.

28/08/04

Chocolate

It's beautiful smooth in texture,
especially when rubbed
on your body,
It's crunchie @ first then
melts in your mouth,
dairy milks is the only one for me,
tomorrow I've got an AA meeting,
shake rattle and roll,
Oh, for a bar I'd sell my soul,
It's nice to receive it
on your birthday,
I'd kill for a chocolate bowl,
Santa Claus, ya bastard,
you ate all my sweets,
just as well, it's Christmas
day, and I'm away to mass,
but when I get back, I'll
get the Easter bunny to
kick your fucking ass,
he'll pull out all your teeth,
and leave them for the fairy,
I'd kill for Sarah's ass,
I'd put it in my pipe and
smoke it with some grass,
they scream it's the ring of fire,
throw her on the pyre,
but that's not fair cos she's so nice,
so, let's rap her up in
sugar and spice.

28/08/04

Coinyabeta

The pleasures of wanking

It's a solitary game,
something like patience,
but if you work too hard,
you'll end up a patient,
It's a fierce boring job, but
some one's got to do it,
a wank's not for Christmas.
It's for the rest of your life,
and you'll have to go solo,
till you find a girl or a wife,
wank with your left,
wank with your right,
be ambidextrous,
and let yourself take flight,
for when you get good,
you learn self-control,
restraint and delivery,
no matter the toll,
so, practice your moves,

let those fingers find their grooves,
like a pianist and his piano,
how funny it is they go together,
if only this feeling could last
Forever!

28/08/04

Group therapy again – We all take a line...

Pourqoui pas

They must be mad,
they know no reason why?
Everyone here is not all bad,
although the doc's all
say we're mad,
we may @ times be quiet sad,
then @ other times fly
that makes us glad,
when all the cards are down,
and the money's in,
frantically swinging
from high to low,
I'm taking to song. So?
Hurry up we've not got
all night Eamonn,
Life is not so shite,
GOODNITE!

28/08/04

Super friend/GRASS

I trust you with my freedom,
in this game, we've chosen to play,
I'm not sure who said the bullshit,
that crime, it does not pay,
He wasn't as good as us,
if that's all he had to say,
Life is good,
we are all sweet,
from the sugar daddy,
to the guy on the street,
but then you turned informer?
Went and got the pigs involved,
Well, I fucking tell u this,
I'll get you when we've revolved,
It's a long road that has no turns,
and then you'll see how it burns,
from friend to fiend,
you only get one chance,
your visas have been revoked,
now you won't get a second glance.

28/08/04

I played group therapy with some of the crew of the Jeanie Johnston when they came and visited me.

Swell Waves

The water that day had
small little ripples,
as I looked on, I could feel
the swell in my nipples,
So, impressed by my breasts,
I decided to show the cripples,
but the wheelchair got in the way,
and with my quiff they
thought I was gay,
as it turned out, they were daft,
and shouted, lob it in there hay!!!
So, I pulled up my pants
and walked away,
to mix with the passengers
was my next intent,
I'll have a few snogs and
make a few sprogs,

was the aim on which
I was hell bent!
But sadly, most of them
ended up being dogs,
then before me was the
angel God sent,
nothing stopped me by
the end I was spent,
but she took me up wrong,
marriage was not what I meant,
but I'm still proud of my bulkhead
with that funny looking dent,
where because of the swell waves,
her head landed two
feet above the vent.

29/08/04

Therapy?

Room with a view
I see an elephant through it,
I'd like to find if this was true,
skip me come back to
me when it's easier,
What amazes me,
the elephant had escaped
from the zoo,
he was a curious creature,
looking for something to do,
turns out not to be true,
but I argue that it is true,
but what do I know?
I live in a shoe,
they've confiscated the laces,
but it doesn't matter,
there ain't no traces,
this evening I'm not at the races,
But I put a few down,
just for the places,
And I couldn't help looking
at all the unfamiliar faces,
For deep down, I felt like
I had all the aces.

30/08/04

The Wagon

The Anti tension,
is like an AA extension,
and the dual diagnosis video,
barely merits a mention,
the Alcohol and Chemical,
Dependence lecture,
could do with some texture,
We need recovery plan groups,
to keep us all interested,
and rally the troops,
And with perseverance,
we'll find our way,
Ni neart go cur le cheile,
Grassy the day,
Sail by your own compass,
till we're finally orientated,
the need to stay on the wagon,
can't be understated!

30/08/04

Weekender Bender

The Ultimate Cyclone,
that's bored us to the bone,
a tough day doing nothing,
3 days rolled into one,
We've had our visitors,
but they've come and gone,
All work stops Friday,
if you work 9 to 5,

little thought of us,
Some distraction to keep us alive,
We're afraid to get too happy,
for fear they'll think we're high,
But we all play our games,
and always on the sly,
And at night, when we're pacing,
that worn path of a corridor,
that the many have them facing,
weekends a weak long,
but drug us enough, and
we mightn't notice,
Sure they'll talk to each other,
and enlighten each other
like the leaf of the lotus,
The best help we get in here,
is the help from each other,
We only need the walls,
To hold up my brother.

31/08/04

NoName

Can you see what I see?
Feel what I feel?
The perception is different,
from one to the next,
it's all in the delivery,
composition of the text,
accent, affliction, affectation,
from the belly past the teeth,
is there any such thing,
as a decorative wreath?
People are dead,
but not forgotten,
is my true belief.
So, I can sit back and relax,
in the quiet satisfaction of my relief.

31/08/04

Scaley

I now do it for me!
And no-one else at all,
Confuse me for you,
After all,
Engage the brain,
Exchange you slayin',
For love and peace,
not out on a lease.

01/09/04

Catharsis

We're all as one,
just moving along,
Everything's going strong,
What's done is gone,
We look to the future,
remember the nice bits of the past,
they remain in our minds,
and forever last,
then monsoon, typhoon,
earthquake,
and tidal wave,
hits our happy home,
Nearly everyone escaped,
but there's one we cannot save,
he's gone with God now,
hangs out with Joey Dunlop,
and the like,
happily doing donuts,
on his new Ducati bike,
So, don't fear his absence,
or reject his presence,
he's just trying to get through,
from him to you,

When it happens again,
relax and take it in,
and the path to healing
will slowly begin.

01/09/04

I ask everyone for a title then squeeze them into a poem. These are the titles given to me…

Kinky sex
Hellfire Club
Mirrors
Always
Shane McGowan
Why me?
Telepathy
Flamboyance

Secret Agent 008

T'was the night pre-discharge,
everyone had the channels,
Ubiquitous to hand,
was always the flannels,
they gathered in a circle,
the shape of a hex,
gathered around,
for some KINKY SEX,
This is the HELLFIRE CLUB,
What's all the noise,
what's the hub,
as he looks in the
MIRRORS for the girls,
he's ALWAYS the same,
Hey you SHANE MCGOWAN,
This is respectable bud!
We love you when you're bowin'?

I'm TELEPATHIC and opaque,
WHY ME?
Says he I spoke to you slowly,
let me be free,
I didn't use too many big words,
yet you didn't listen,
you shower of turds,
So, to you and your order,
with FLAMBOYANCE
reach around,
to your heinous anus,
and stick it up to the border,
I see your reaction,
authoritarian at all cost,
well out of my way,
you're about to be bossed!

01/09/04

The 32 Musketeers

Optical illusion,
injection or extrusion,
Subliminal hit,
One slight of the hand flit,
See what you perceive,
but don't always believe,
misdirection is open,
so keep on groping,
we can make it as one,
All or none,
One for ye all,
and all of ye for one.

01/09/04

The bullshit I was told

(Medication)
They're sugar coated candy,
for your pleasure,
but not just your own,
they elevate, deflate, annihilate,
whatever your head has grown,
So down the hatch,
without a scratch,
make sure and lick the bowl,
cos these smarties have the answer,
to the question in your soul.

01/09/04

You are all @ sea

At the end of the phone,
is the end of that line,
but it's the start of another,
a magnificent maze for a mind,
dig out the truth,
from underneath your feet,
the soil is soft,
waiting to meet and greet,
to answer the question,
of the struggling fleet,
so, with a lick of paint,
to make the accountants faint,
cos a half-measure man I ain't,
Sunrise to Sunset,
the fleet will sail proud,
and from over their eyes,
remove the shrouds.

02/09/04

I asked the three ladies for a title each. This what they gave me…
blowjobs
holiday in the sun
miss sixty shoes

3's

What sort of job do you need,
to pay for those shoes?
Whatever, you need a holiday,
to get rid of all those blues,
Your tongue must be numb,
after all those blows,
you need Miss sixty shoes,
to go in those clothes,
Sketchers are cool,
blowjobs are better,
even tastier they are,
without a French letter!!!

02/09/04

KowLOonKrazy

Let's meet @ high noon,
any earlier is too soon,
and when we kick your ass,
You can pick up those jaws of glass,
Well fuck you,
I'll just do,
that sliver really brings
out your eyes,
Fooled you all along,
I was Bruce lee in disguise,
right here in the hospital,,
hiding under the mats,
bequeathing your suicide prize!

02/09/04

Teamwork

Sure I'll do it myself,
I trust no-one else,
if ye want a job done right,
Ye do it yourself.
That's the attitude,
that won't get you far in life,
Job, holiday, money or,
maybe not even a
husband or a wife,
Feeding off each other,
like the carnivores we are,
munching on all knowledge,
from a distant and afar,
pursue the pursuit,
of the words from the Jesuit,
about working together,
and getting along,
doing the right thing,
and not the favourable wrong.

02/09/04

Tree-leaves

Does leaves leave a tree,
or a tree leaves a leaves?
They're parting company together,
from tree to leave and
your tree to leave,
Where the wind blows,
will keep you on your toes,
from noon day sun,
to frigid night has begun,
so go, young one,
find your own shelter,
may your life be like everyone,
Helter Skelter!!!

03/09/04

10/1

That time already?
5/1 now!
They're falling steady,
but bouncing back up,
I'm not known,
where to stand?
lookout below,
here comes the band.

03/09/04

Autumn

Spring forward,
fall back,
the cycle of life,
is on its perpetual track,
to sleep the sleep,
of a thousand years,
and wake when winters,
thawed from our fears,
the fall of a leaf,
spreading seed where it lands,
the Glory of life,
is in your God given hand.

03/09/04

Children

From infancy to infamy,
kids are born without sin,
So, the habits we give them,
always sink in,
Be good to your child,
because one day they'll
be in your shoes,

and need to retrieve from
their memories,
your valid views,
Kids are cool,
from the mouths of babes,
Caught many a fool,
we thought were Lincoln Abes,
My Father always says,
that he personally wears,
his inner child on the outside,
if it bothers some people,
He does say, who cares?
But my Ma always says,
I never grew out of the
terrible two's,
but there's a lot of us out there,
Don't hide yourself away,
and you will not lose.

03/09/04

Clingy

I apologize not!
For what I'll do,
I'll stick to your mind,
like sniffing super glue,
breathing straight to the brain,
through all barriers of pain,
picking up things,
You never knew,
Next thing you're saying it,
Straight from the heart,
when it's fabricated lunacy,
with the stench of a fart,
so, gather up your
mind's belongings,
while they're still intact,
start the revolution now,
not after the fact!

03/09/04

Little Hitleress

What's the fucking story?
What is it with you today?
Did I do something wrong?
And I'm being punished
in this way?
If I did, it wasn't intentional,
but where the Jesus are we,
A facility for correctional?!

03/09/04

Sexually frustrated

Not even a fondle,
a feel in the dark,
the tiniest of touches,
as small as a quark?
Pourquoi pas?
Oh, la la!

05/09/04

Bog roll blues

Dysphoric constipation,
deep within my bowel,
if only I could scrape it out,
with the mathematician's trowel,
the pen may be mightier
than the sword,
but the pencil is best of all,
because once prepared,
it'll write in the sun and
even in rainfall,
with friends like you,
Mr. Vindaloo,
who needs enemas,

just for me findaloo,
colonic irrigation,
that's nutritious too!

05/09/04

¶'s

Crossing the eyes,
is a great disguise,
so, the doctors and nurses,
who are thrifty with their purses,
and run a tight ship,
from the tip to their lip,
can give great analyzation,
of our personal mojo,
and our verbal incontinence,
will fade into the past distance.

05/09/04

Paperback

Within these paper walls,
I learned not to trip,
on the pride that falls,
it has my ego contained,
my elation restrained,
and all of my faculties,
healthfully sustained.

05/09/04

Sarah

Sitting in the evening sun,
adjusting as it slowly fades away,
and relaxing in the
definite assurance,
that tomorrow is another day,
the cool of the night comes in,
gently washing over your skin,
as the ends of today's
thoughts begin,
and the beginning of
yesterday's thoughts sink in,
Agitated, irritated, complicated,
frustrated, fat, ugly,
and to top it off,
over compensated,
with something totally unrelated,
I wish I had some proper drugs,
that would leave me fine,
and gently sedated.

06/09/04

C'est la vie

There's no fault,
There's no blame,
everything is as it was,
it's all the same,
Pain follows pleasure,
as night follows day,
it may take a while,
but you'll soon again say hooray,
Drop the guard for a second,
on unfounded trust,
so, learn the lesson again,
if you must then you must,
The trusts still there,
but in a different way,
c'est meilleur,
I have to say.

06/09/04

Musique

Let it run through your
body,
let it run through your
veins,
Let it gallop unleashed,
through the cells of your brains,
riveted to your seat,
ecstatically static,
or jumping ecstatic to the
beat,
joyfully bouncing off the walls,
God, what a treat,
you've given us this
gift,
of overall expression,
it can cause lovers to love,
an amends to rifts,
and lift depression.

06/09/04

Turbulence

The early worm,
Catches the flight,
destination unknown,
what's the movie on
the menu tonight?
Then it feels the crunch,
and begins to squirm,
the feeling of dread,
travels from tail to head,
high it glides,
through the early morning light,
the landing pad of the nest,
is now in sight,
the hungriest of the chicks,
is always fed last,
the loudest of them all,
stands proud and tall,
pushes the rest aside,
who are left to fast,
but the others learn a lesson,
of how to survive.
to hold the roof,
and we give the cold shoulder
to those who are aloof.

07/09/04

Focus

Hearts and minds will meet as one,
agreeing there is more,
on its way with morning sun,
comes the daily chore,
a grind of the mind,
the unbegrudging kind,
as we peel the orange skin rind,
to cure the blind,

And blind they are and
deaf and dumb,
by accident or choice,
they lost their sense and confidence.
they failed to find their voice,
they will search, and they will find.
some billion screams,
the voice of one,
throughout their dreams.
The volume of their unison,
will wake them from their slumber.
with the sun on the horizon,
they'll show us their true number.

07/09/04

King prawns

Don't blame it on me,
Don't blame it on the moonlight,
Don't blame it on the good times,
blame it on the loony,
Big wheels keep on turning,
does your conscience bother you?
Clear you mind,
absolve your sins,
Step aside,
we're coming through,
you're either for us,
or against,
You decide,
Cause we're about to conquer,
then divide,
By peaceful means and
forceful ways,
so tomorrow can be
everybody's today,
AND SO SAY
ALL OF
ME!

08/09/04

I asked 5 people for a title each. This is the result…
Beach
Friendship
Loyalty
Predictability
Trippin

Five

Lying in the sand as far
as the eye can see,
hot to touch, the water's
far to reach,
I'll run with light feet,
on this crowded BEACH,
when I threw the party,
I thought I'd get a few,
I could never have
imagined with a whip,
I'd have so many people,
to honour me with their
FRIENDSHIP,
They're here for a good
time, not a long time,
embarrassed as I am,
they treat me like royalty,
pledge their honour and support,
and give me their LOYALTY,
People are cool and all like variety,
a certain askewness and
respectability,
that's a mile from the norm,
and only when needed then
PREDICTABILITY,
the fires lit,
and the bar-b's on,
those slices of new life,
we'll soon be flippin,
and a perspective that's
now needed,
cause reality is TRIPPIN!

08/09/04

Hear & Now

Where am I?
Am I here?
I know I am,
but others fear,
but don't worry ma,
because I do listen to you,
don't think I ignore,
because I do what I do,
I'll take it handy,
keep the head,
but people piss me off,
and I see the mist of red,
this does not mean,
that I am still high,
but the apron strings need cut,
I need to fly,
so, I ask you please,
it's hard enough,
let me go,
and find my way outta the rough.

08/09/04

Nail on the head

The do's and don'ts,
of life's wants,
Will they?
Won't they?
Don't they know, hey?
It's their hay day,
Do it now,
before it's too late,
don't look to other people,
2 judge your mental state,
be yourself off the shelf,
and sometimes off the wall,
Stand tall and be proud,
because you are
answering your call.

08/09/04

I was having fun...

Snakes & Dragons

To come here in the first place
was a beautiful mistake,
for the first time in my life,
I've let the Dragon eat the Snake,
It squirmed,
it wormed,
it tried to wriggle, it's way free,
but the Dragon had a grip on it,
better than me,
so tight it'll hold,
never to unfold,
till the day I die,
or at least till I'm old,
Unforeseen friendships,
forged for the future fate,
late night discussions,
where we all debate,
It's a big discussion,
So, call it a mass debate,
where we all come together,
and demonstrate,
our cunning linguistics
are plain to see,
the sides to the argument
are always three,
triangulation,
has so many uses,
from navigation to fire,

combine them all together for
navigation with higher fire,
Higher than life,
is not a possible state,
neither is perfection,
but I'm coming close at this rate,
I've met so many people,
now true friends of mine,
whom I'd sit in any company,
with non-alcoholic wine,
They're smart,
they're funny,
and so god damned good looking,
they all just ooze charisma,
that would have jealous
people puking.
But I'm one of them,
so it's not us that has the problem,
it's you with your glue,
trying to stick labels
on us like them.

09/09/04

Windolay

Dampened by curtains,
lies the direct sunlight,
So, pull back the veils,
and view the sight,
Where shadows in the room,
go from merged as one,
to individualistic outlines,
cast by the sun,
The window sees all,
without and within,
when viewed from the outside,
a sneak peek is not a sin,
curiosity that's common,
to all of us,
the glass goes both ways,
so, there is no fuss.

09/09/04

Animals

Neanderthal to homo-sapien,
Darwin's theory seems to fit,
The evidence is there,
where the first fire was lit,
Gavin said to me,
of all the people he'd like to meet,
was the guy who stole the flame,
from underneath the
great Gods feet,
Evolution started somewhere,
but as animals some think it was us,
What about the mammals
and birds and fish,
it's the superior attitude
that's causing all the fuss,
Global warming and extinction,
both go hand and hand,
the ivory tusks in South Arica,
for less than a couple of Rand,
Leopard skin rugs, polar bear coats,
only the Eskimos have those rights,
and those indigenous
to the native land,
who have the foresight,
they don't kill the young,
before they procreate,
only the homo-sapiens
whites do that,
and use another as bait,
two birds with one stone,
It's not how they should see,
It's pretty obvious to me,
Is it obvious to ye?

09/09/04

Lost in Music

The void is filled,
with waves on the air,
penetrating, bouncing,
without a care,
follow the sound,
but where does it come from?
Without vents to the medium,
there'd be no hum de
da de da hum,
We'd wander around aimlessly,
So, thank God for atmosphere,
who cares where it ends or starts,
We can get lost in music right here.

10/09/04

A kiss

What's in a question?
All the time.
Why's always there,
in the meaning of rhyme,
itch the scratch,
and scratch the itch,
is a kiss a kiss,
without a hitch,
some can't differentiate,
for them life's a bitch,
the grey area's blue,
and it makes them see red,
black at night,
but sometimes white instead,
yet for those that know,
it's simple and sweet,
it's lips and minds,
just happening to meet.

10/09/04

Confidence

Does a do don't,
When a will won't?
Of course, it will,
a do does when it don't,
even when it won't,
I will!

10/09/04

In-between Dreams

There's too much time,
Spent between dreams,
even if they come true,
time spent planning,
anticipating,
time spent on a fair few,
and sometimes time,
between dreams,
lasts longer than they
last themselves,
and it extends,
to such extent that,
There are dreams no longer,
without any themes,
that makes ya stronger,
Strength of mind,
and courage of conviction,
Dreams that'll last,
from the obscurest prediction.

10/09/04

Psychiatric hospital

It's a meeting of minds,
friendship in steel binds,
We're all the same,
So, there's no-one to blame,
and if you can't see that,
then you're fucking blind.

Quotes

"I have been underestimated
for decades. I've done
very well that way."
- Helmut Kohl. German Chancelor

"When I was first here, we
had the advantages of the
underdog. Now we have the
disadvantages of the overdog."
- Abba Eban

"Sell your soul to yourself. You'll
make more money that way."
- Marilyn Monroe

"I'm talking to myself again
but I think I'm getting
through this time."

"Idea's are more powerful than
guns. We do not allow our
enemies to guns, why should
we allow them to have ideas?"
- Joe Stalin

10/09/04

Road rage

Give them all a cage,
to vent off the rage,
and a wheel that won't squeal,
and maybe the echo,
will let them see what we feel,
And how they show themselves up
on life's stage.

11/09/04

Should....

Should I rest?
Should I try my best?
Should I shine?
Should I have some wine?
Should I read?
Should I speak out loud?
Should I come down?
Should I descend from the cloud?
Should I float?
Should I stand?
Should I take a boat?
Should I land?
Should I walk?
Should I run?
Should I spread the word?
Should I smoke the gun?
Should I test?
Should I jest?
Should I just wait?
Should the time come.

11/09/04

Fingers

I found the solution,
but what's the problem?
The question's in the answer,
variety solves them,
Now you have the information,
use it wisely,
Unequivocal,
And don't be miserly,
talk till understood,
under whatever they stand,
Q and A sessions,
to beat the band,
Animalistically humble,
with a giggly growl,
laugh or maul,
on the benevolent prowl.

12/09/04

Alien Nation

A terrorist state to be in,
Fear across the nation,
It's the deliberation of this
deleterious delinquent,
that causes the frustration,
it's their need to understand,
Why not let me be?
Leave me alone I'm grand,
So, fuck you all,
get me or don't,
I'll lose no life nor sleep,
if you do or won't.

12/09/04

Chair

Bouncing as he learns
his first word,
and smiles his first smile,
sitting up high as he learns,
to feed himself this growing child,
tall enough to sit in front,
seatbelt on,
sit up straight,
first day in class,
no comfort here, but new
friends are great,
waiting for trial,
juvenile thief and mother tense,
"Take a seat,"
"Take the weight of your feet,"
"Sit there till you get some sense."
We'll make it understandable
and concise,
not long till it'll condense,
now sit on your throne,
but listen to advise,
your vocation and rightful place,
after all, it costs nothing to be nice.

12/09/04

CONformity

Is this what normal is
supposed to be?
Boredom x boredom x
10 to the 6 times 3,
they don't lighten your mood,
they try to extinguish your flare,
because for their closed
minds and blind eyes,

it's too much glare,
well, frankly, my dear people,
I don't fucking care,
Here I am,
take me as I come,
grandiose plans or not,
they'll put me number 1.

12/09/04

Random Rodent

All over the place,
just like a rat race,
no direction known,
but full of Grace,
delightfully gliding,
sense of smell guiding,
never to end or fail,
at the end of the tale.

12/09/04

Words

Unequivocally speaking,
Double entendre intended,
Speaking from the brain,
cos my heart says spend it,
Use the words you know,
learn a new one each day,
fear not people's ignorance,
no matter what they say,
don't dumb down,
cause of who's listening in,
your words and your
implementation,
Whether pencil, pen or pin,
Plan what you're saying off the cuff,
know where to end and
where to begin,
If they don't understand or won't,
cause enough is enough,
well, that's their tough.

13/09/04

Old and why's?

If youth is wasted on the young,
then surely air is wasted
on the lung,
From the old and wise,
To the young and the why's?
Cloak and dagger,
fear of knowledge to impart,
Cos if you tell me too much,
I might know more than you,
you old fart,
Knowledge is the fodder,
that makes kids minds broader,
It's the name of the game,
to teach what we learn,
for some kids, it's a chore,
for other's they yearn,
So tell what you know,
cos there's no better feeling,
than watching them grow
and their young mind
hit the ceiling.

13/09/04

I was released for the night and met this lovely lady Farrell. I asked her was she in any relation?

Susie

When I saw the tassles shake,
My brain applied lusts brake,
But the more I watched,
the more I admired,
lust took over,
as my brain was inspired,
a kiss on the lips,
from those tassled hips,
cigarettes tossed aside,
passion surpassing,
the will to hide,
the dance floor we'll clear,
as we seek, hide, and glide.

13/09/04

The Angelus

The bell tolls for whom,
like a hot air ballon,
till I'm blue in the face,
it's a marathon race,
26 miles with my sandals on,
How many miles to Babylon?
I believe in the truth,
In all shapes and forms strewth,
Away with the lies,
and those lying eyes,
Cut the crap,
and show me where it's at,
Some regime to uphold,
So my mind won't be bold,
13 months now, and
you're still not sure,
It seems you've decided retention
is better than cure.

14/09/04

Elationships

Hi, how are ye?
How's it going, hi?
Pleased to meet you,
I'm doing fine,
what's your favourite colour?
Blue like the skies,
same as meself,
I've got a head for heights,
but I'm partial to brown,
sort of like the earth,
very deep down,
in a way it's parallel,
yet we physically touch,
on a molecular level,
not for the impaired
of vision as such,
meetings of minds,
of all different kinds,
we've broken them up,
is it ourselves we applaud,
but who are we,
to sit and play God?

14/09/04

The Wild bunch

With a bang and a crunch,
before and after lunch,
It begins as we wake,
and shape our thoughts with a rake,
run our fingers through our hair,
pretending we care,
Vociferous in nature,
Colossus in stature,
Assimilated and combined,

individualistically entwined,
as the day flows,
our cognitive grows,
agitated, aggravated, bolchy,
sympathetic, realistic, ballistic,
from our stratospheric head
to out magma toes,
Philosophy, mathematics,
University of life,
We eat Geo-politics,
without even a scrunch of strife,
So, try your tactics,
cos to us it's tic-tacs,
you may think you're smart,
but this is only the start,
we haven't even begun,
on a count of three,
We haven't even reached one,
Conquer after divide,
you better run and hide,
we see your intentions,
before your thoughts collide,
Solidarity is key,
but nature finds a way,
we may piss you off,
but our future's ours together,
into the fray.

16/09/04

Dog

Man's best friend,
or only for a lend,
unconditional love from below,
hail, rain, shine or snow,
Gran's companion,
or Belzebub's minion,
Comfort for the night,
Or source of tremendous fright,
teeth bared when they want to,
bites worse than its bark,
loyal with every fibre of it's being,
to the smallest quark,
Shapes and sizes varying,
and temperaments likewise,
howling, growling, prowling,
but see the trust that's in their eyes,
hunting, grunting, ferreting out,
smelling danger before
it comes near,
Hearing the signals,
that we fear to hear.

16/09/04

Leaving

I caught it,
I got it,
It was the last one I looked at,
I should've looked there first,
I've made it now in seconds flat,
leaving the craic behind,
but it's only the start of
what's to come,
it's the top rung of one ladder,
and the bottom of another one,
these are ladders without snakes
to bring you undone,
they cleanse with each step,
a filtration system that's
second to none,
so, we are never leaving,
just enjoy life's journey of fun!

16/09/04

When I get out

It's past the stage,
Where we're at the last page,
So, it's fucking me off,
I'm still in this cage,
They've neither seen me at my best,
or in a fit of rage,
but keep finding reasons
to keep me,
It'll be earth quaking proportions
on a Richter gauge!

17/09/04

Revelation

Footprints glowing,
as my mind keeps growing,
the path ever changing,
the distance ever ranging,
360's the direction,
no need for election,
outside's the insides reflection,
and it remains the same
on closer inspection,
A heartfelt search,
idiosyncratic research,
absolved of my sins,
regaining my wings and my fins,
for the journey that lies before me,
through land and sea,
sounds and snow follow me,
I'm starting to see,
the woods and the tree,
the one hand clapping,
without flapping or slapping,
it fell without noise,
it fell without noise,
and thankfully missed me.

17/09/04

SandyAndy

Like a fox,
She walks,
Without a care,
stops for nothing,
a shout of "who goes there?!"
She's SandyAndy,
with the lustrous coloured hair,
a sheen and shine,
and a smile that would win,
an attractive face,
with the fluff on her chin,
From a shaky start,
with the pound as a home,
to a dwelling place,
She can call her own,
lady of the manor,
her slender long legs stride,
with a tail like a gown,
that shows her assurance,
not her pride,
She's an equal in the family,
So, don't forget,
she's one of you,
not just a pet.

17/09/04

Associates

Claude Monet paints a picture,
Arethra breathes a tune,
Is it a reflection of light
on the window,
or is it the Moon?
Would within woods,
he touches with his moods,

Television dormant, nearly extinct,
not too many strokes,
always succinct,
14 and 3 tables,
a dozen vacant for the disciples,
to recount their parables and fables,
Cigar smoke fills the air,
invoking memories of
when I was there,
Creating the atmosphere required,
for Arethra and Monet,
and me a Robbie,
to chill the night away.

17/09/04

I asked for 6 titles and this is what they gave me…
inspiration
the eternal divine love of Christ on the Crucifix
Duty
trust
friendship
truth

Doggerel

Try to separate them,
it's an illusion,
emotion and intellect,
will cause confusion,
INSPIRATION from happiness,
and from the wound the dog licks,
THE ETERNAL DIVINE
LOVE OF CHRIST ON
THE CRUCIFIX,
Your DUTY to uphold,
and delegation to observe,
the language has been spoken,
now let them earn the
TRUST that they deserve,
FRIENDSHIP first and foremost,
and a TRUTH that'll never swerve.

18/09/04

Comply

Slow up,
Slow down,
round and round,
the cage must open,
before I drown,
thoughts slowing,
then racing,
but always faster than yours,
so, you'll never understand,
give you a 3rd degree,
and you still won't see,
because you're not me.

LETTERKENNY MENTAL ASYLUM IN DONEGAL

14/02/02

Lazers

The water in the waves,
the boat's in the raves,
reviews and views,
give wind to the pews,
religion to some,
amalgamate the lot,
from yachting like lazers,
to Superyachtings plot,
Merchant, Fishing,
Seagulls in flight,
If you see the birds,
go on your might,
heading in land,
sign of a storm,
the water around the boats,
below the Seagull birds,
give the wind gorm.

07/09/17

Fiona

I saw your thought,
I saw your mind,
Unfettered, Unfeathered,
beautiful smile.

22/01/18

I thought of Nostradamus and how I always wanted to be an Astronaut growing up.

Astronautadamus

Flying in space,
the view of the world,
the heat of the sun,
can be visually heard,
floating spaced out,
I'm staring into,
Chinese wall,
lights of the cities,
stars either side,
above and below,
cloud cover over,
rain to the right,
Sun to the left,
snow above and below,
the equator is tightening its belt,
the change in the
environment is felt,
birds singing earlier,
loggers and miners,
are becoming ever warier,
beaches with leeches,
sucking the energy dry,
locusts on the land,
and now on the sea.
What has to be done to set us free?
Learn the culture,
don't muscle in,
Getting it wrong,
should be a sin.

26/03/18

Mother

It seems my veins come and go,
depending on the flow,
When people bite in,
I feel the squelch,
their thoughts and dreams,
are in my mind,
I bite back,
it gives me power,
Woman cave,
and give me their flowers,
Men abound,
on the ground,
everyone looking to stomp,
It's fucking me off,
I'm starting to cough,
and I don't need that,
to give me attention,
Sitting at the fire,
they're all on the pyre,
Who the fuck is on my side?
They're all out judging,
and reputation smudging,
and my friends are worse
than my Mother!

26/03/18

Darkness

The darkness fall,
it causes a speed,
of day leering into the night,
the closing of doors,
just like the moors,
of myself about to take flight,
the rev of an engine nowhere
that can be seen,
cock hanging in the wind,
Seahorses everywhere,
But my mother doesn't
seem to care,
Antibes doesn't loathe me,
they were out to scare,
well, I'm in bed in the
community's care.

23/10/18

Happy BD Andrew

Circular living,
in halls that are square,
Smoking for social,
detention that's not fair,
Drinking unavailable,
but we still have the craic,
boring as fuck,
monotony's back,
Table tennis,
ping and the pong,
we're only in here,
because of what we did wrong,
Tourettes?
What's the bets,
that you're gonna be cured,
it's your birthday today,
and you can cry if you want to,
all your cairde are here,
and they are all sincere.

23/10/18

Timo

Tim hovers,
he hoots,
he bangs his boots,
looking for attention,
but love is at the roots.

23/10/18

With Ease

Woods for the mood,
creameries behind you,
planting the seeds,
for new growing life,
bopping to the music,
the reigning champ,
table tennis pastime,
could be a ramp,
professional player,
or even semi-pro,
a new future ahead of you,
forget about the blow.

LIMERICKS

14/08/04

Vomit

That was the vomit of a comet,
look at the trail that was on it!
You can tell by the smell,
that it came straight from hell,
and there were clearly
some carrots upon it!

14/08/04

Fish

Two fish in a tank,
having a reach around wank,
Then one turns to the other,
and says, "Aren't you, my brother?",
"Well, if you can't thank me,
who can you thank?"

14/08/04

Food

Are we consumed by food?
All our resilience stolen
by some hood?
Or compressed in a box,
with very fat blocks,
then eat depending on the mood?

14/08/04

Journey

I'm on a Kama Sutra journey,
but with my KY,
it won't be burny,
we'll entangle like contortionist,
inverted mime expressionists,
all on our Island of Alderney.

14/08/04

Actors

I think that actor James
Dean was gay,
and to get his arse wellied,
he did pay,
His motorbike was an
extension to his dick,
and a shitty ring piece he did lick,
And he widened the circle
of his friends that way.

14/08/04

Animal

In bed, I'm described as an animal,
Cos my intuition is
almost subliminal,
And as I give them what they want,
we've got a jolly old jaunt,
and she gasps for air like a mammal.

14/08/04

Director

I think that gay James Dean
was an actor,
and to keep an eye on his hole,
he used a protractor,
right down to the butt-plugs,
what a whiff,
and that lovely gay Elvis quiff!
He should have forgotten
about the Harley,
and drove a tractor.

www.ingramcontent.com/pod-product-compliance
Lightning Source LLC
Chambersburg PA
CBHW060403080526
44583CB00012B/456